WRITING THAT MATTERS

WRITING THAT MATTERS

A HANDBOOK FOR CHICANX & LATINX STUDIES

L HEIDENREICH AND
RITA E. URQUIJO-RUIZ

THE UNIVERSITY OF
ARIZONA PRESS
TUCSON

The University of Arizona Press
www.uapress.arizona.edu

We respectfully acknowledge the University of Arizona is on the land and territories of Indigenous peoples. Today, Arizona is home to twenty-two federally recognized tribes, with Tucson being home to the O'odham and the Yaqui. Committed to diversity and inclusion, the University strives to build sustainable relationships with sovereign Native Nations and Indigenous communities through education offerings, partnerships, and community service.

ISBN-13: 978-0-8165-4267-3 (paperback)
ISBN-13: 978-0-8165-5290-0 (ebook)

Cover design by Leigh McDonald
Cover art by Anel I. Flores / www.anelflores.com
Interior illustrations by Anel I. Flores
Designed and typeset by Sara Thaxton in 10.5/14 Warnock Pro with Lulo and Helvetica Neue LT Std

Publication of this book is made possible in part by the proceeds of a permanent endowment created with the assistance of a Challenge Grant from the National Endowment for the Humanities, a federal agency.

Library of Congress Cataloging-in-Publication Data
Names: Heidenreich, L, 1964– author. | Urquijo-Ruiz, Rita, author.
Title: Writing that matters : a handbook for Chicanx and Latinx studies / L Heidenreich and Rita E. Urquijo-Ruiz.
Other titles: Handbook for Chicanx and Latinx studies
Description: Tucson : University of Arizona Press, 2024. | Includes bibliographical references and index.
Identifiers: LCCN 2023031918 (print) | LCCN 2023031919 (ebook) | ISBN 9780816542673 (paperback) | ISBN 9780816552900 (ebook)
Subjects: LCSH: Academic writing—Handbooks, manuals, etc. | Hispanic Americans—Study and teaching—Handbooks, manuals, etc. | LCGFT: Handbooks and manuals.
Classification: LCC E184.S75 H45 2024 (print) | LCC E184.S75 (ebook) | DDC 808.02/08968—dc23/eng/20230912
LC record available at https://lccn.loc.gov/2023031918
LC ebook record available at https://lccn.loc.gov/2023031919

Printed in the United States of America
♾ This paper meets the requirements of ANSI/NISO Z39.48-1992 (Permanence of Paper).

CONTENTS

ACKNOWLEDGMENTS

Because Writing Is a Collective Activity

We owe a debt to the many people who made it possible for us to craft this handbook. One of the first communities to come to mind is the people of Mujeres Activas en Letras y Cambio Social (MALCS). We were fortunate to receive their critical input and remain grateful that our colegas, comadres, and compañer@s have supported and nurtured us throughout our careers. It is at the Summer Institute that we were/are able to breathe, receive mentorship, and eventually mentor others.

I was fortunate to receive a research fellowship from the Center for the Humanities at Washington State University during the fall of 2020. This allowed me to conduct research for my manuscript project on the women of the United Farm Workers, and also to continue working on this manuscript. Because the COVID pandemic created extra family responsibilities for me, I would not have been able to continue work on either project without that institutional support. Experiencing family loss during this time, I also appreciate the patience of the University of Arizona Press, especially Kristen Buckles, as I worked to get back into working order.

I am also grateful to my writing partners: both Dr. Rita E. Urquijo-Ruiz and Dr. Beth Buyserie. Knowing that when I log on (at 6:30 a.m.) I will find a welcoming face looking out from my screen keeps me stumbling out of bed to write every Monday and Friday morning. I am thankful to Amy Sharpe of the Women's Center for creating and sustaining a safe space for women-of-color students and for being a friend through the ups and downs of working at a public university, and to my social justice and COJ buds at Sacred Heart (I will make it back to meetings eventually) for keeping me grounded. For her patience with my long writing hours, I am eternally grateful to my spouse, Karen Gallaghar. Writing is, indeed, a community experience, and I cannot do it without you.

—L Heidenreich

I am grateful to my dear family members in both México and the United States. To friends, colegas, and mentors for your continuous support. For your indefatigable dedication and patience, dear L, un millón de gracias. I am proud of our collaborations, but I am especially grateful for our decades of friendship y tanto cariño. Marisela "Sela" Chávez, thank you, love, for showing me a kinder and gentler way of being in this world. Te amo tanto, tanto. The year 2022 took away our furry loves Ori and Tin Tin, who kept us company for 13.5 and 16.5 years, respectively. Perrótoro and Perrítiri, we love you and miss you every day. Gracias for being such loving limalís and perfect writing companions. To our editor extraordinaire, Kristen Buckles, our sincerest gratitude for following Gloria E. Anzaldúa's advice to always "do work that matters." In memory of all our loved ones who transitioned out of this physical world, pero especialmente a mi prima Blanca Judith Ruíz Olivas.

—Rita E. Urquijo-Ruiz

Together, we are also grateful to our manuscript reviewers. While we may never know who you are, we appreciate how your critiques helped us to dramatically improve our work. Our sincere appreciation to the folks at University of Arizona Press for your dedication to this project. Thanks also to Dr. Eddy Francisco Alvarez, Jr., who took time to read through the penultimate draft, and to Anel I. Flores for agreeing to craft the beautiful images found in this volume as well as the cover. Of course, there are many other folks who supported us and touched our lives while we were working on this text. The pandemic was an immense time of loss, and we would not have come through the last few years with healthy spirits if not for the support of numerous family, colegas, and friends. ¡Mil gracias!

L Heidenreich, Pullman, Washington
Rita E. Urquijo-Ruiz, San Antonio, Texas

WRITING THAT MATTERS

Introduction

I Crush the Patriarchy with My Scholarship and Writing

> I crush the patriarchy by leaving a seed of consciousness behind at every space that I navigate. I crush the patriarchy all the times that I'm the first trans Latina to speak at an event or a school, which is often. I crush the patriarchy by ensuring that I'm not the last trans Latina to have these talks. I make sure the people in my community also hold the keys to crush the systems that keep us down, in place and silent. We all have some truth to speak.
>
> — ISA NOYOLA IN *LATINA MAGAZINE*, 2016

> Who gave us permission to perform the act of writing? Why does writing seem so unnatural for me? I'll do anything to postpone it. . . . The voice recurs in me: *Who am I, a poor Chicanita from the sticks, to think I could write?* Why am I compelled to write? . . . Because the world I create in the writing compensates for what the real world does not give me. By writing I put order in the world, give it a handle so I can grasp it. . . . To show that I *can* and that I *will* write. . . . I write because I'm scared of writing, but I'm more scared of not writing.
>
> — GLORIA EVANGELINA ANZALDÚA,
> "SPEAKING IN TONGUES," 1981

The ability and privilege to write, research, and speak our truths is an extraordinary honor that brings with it a profound responsibility. As college and university students you have the opportunity to gain the tools to write, research, and speak in ways that empower yourself and (y)our communities. You can learn to strengthen yourself, to crush the patriarchy, and to inspire the next generation of writers-activists. Our goal with this handbook is to guide you in becoming a brave researcher, confident writer, and valuable member of your communities. Whether this handbook was assigned to you by an instructor or you picked it up when browsing the shelves at your bookstore or library, we hope it helps you excel in your writing and research courses and inspires you to use these skills to give back to (y)our communities, and to create a better, more just world.

As first-generation Chicana and Chicanx queer scholars and professors, we, your authors, have worked in the fields of Chicanx and Latinx studies, as well as in LGBTQIA+ or "jotería" studies, for over two decades. Rita E. Urquijo-Ruiz, author of *Wild Tongues: Transnational Mexican Popular Culture* and co-editor of five additional books, and L Heidenreich, author of *"This Land Was Mexican Once": Histories of Resistance from Northern California* and *Nepantla²: Transgender Mestiz@ Histories in Times of Global Shift*, are established teachers and writers in Chicanx and Latinx studies. We remember, however, what it feels like to sit at a desk learning the tools of our respective fields of literature and history with texts primarily written from Eurocentric, heteronormative, and settler-colonial perspectives. As teachers, we understand the struggle to make meaning from such texts and/or to develop our own writing from scratch using materials that are alienating to us as first-generation students, professors, and authors. We understand that Black, Brown, Indigenous, and other people of color (BBIPOC) consistently have difficulties surviving and thriving in academia due to its inherent racist, Eurocentric, heteronormative, and classist culture. Therefore, we crafted this book to be used with other tools to support you as you progress through your university or college experience.

Because higher education was not designed with us in mind, when we, with much family and community support, make it to a community college, a four-year college, or a university, it is imperative, as queer Chicana author Cherríe Moraga encourages us, to create our own "familia from scratch" in such places.[1] Once

we find our networks of support among faculty, staff, other students, and alumni, surviving and thriving is possible. With the
affirming encouragement of our academic familia, becoming a
strong writer/researcher gets easier as we continue to fend off
"impostor syndrome" and other academic insecurities imposed
on us. This handbook seeks to be the one we needed or desired
as undergraduate students back in the 1980s and '90s. We recognize that decades later, much remains the same in academia, and
we know you/we still need a book like this one, which reflects
(y)our communities of color as communities of scholars with
unlimited saberes/knowledges. It is our obligation, as Noyola
and Anzaldúa state, to give ourselves permission to crush the patriarchy by triumphing over our fear of writing. We, "little Chi-
canitas/Chicanitos/Chicanxs from the sticks" and others, will be
the ones to create the world our communities have envisioned.

Our handbook was born from our own conversations with
each other as we complained yearly about how alienating the
writing manuals are for students, especially first-generation
Black, Indigenous, Brown, and queer students of color, in our
classes. Additionally, it includes the many lessons we developed
for our writing courses throughout the years, as well as tools we
gained from a workshop with the scholar-activists of Mujeres
Activas en Letras y Cambio Social (MALCS), a national organization of Chicana/Latina/Afrolatina/Indigenous women and
gender-nonconforming individuals that focuses on our fields
of study through scholarship, community art, and activism. As
noted by Karen Mary Davalos, Chicana and Latina feminist writing and production is collaborative—we do not work in isolation.[2] This handbook was not written in isolation. Your own best
work will not be written in isolation.

While ours is the first handbook of its kind in this century, it
is not the first one historically. We are influenced by the work of
Irene Isabel Blea, who in 1995 created a handbook that centered
Chicanx communities in the work we do. She mapped the influ-

FIGURE 1 Writing is a community activity.

ence of Chicana feminist scholarship on the field and insisted that Chicano studies (as it was called then) must excavate, make visible, and analyze those places where "race, class, and gender converge" to shape both the past and the present.[3] Blea insisted that scholars be aware of and take into consideration our own social locations and biases, and that we consistently approach our work in relation to our communities as we give back to them.[4] We hope to honor Blea's work by mapping the many ways in which Chicana/Chicano/Chicanx studies has developed and evolved over the decades, examining the manner in which Latinx studies emerged and, at times, converged with Chicanx studies; we hope to offer the tools that today are critical for scholars in our interrelated and often overlapping fields of study.

From Colonialism, Resistance

Latinx history and culture have deep roots in the soil of the Americas—roots that precede the arrival of European settlers to the land. This intricate history can make it difficult to choose a point of origin—a starting place from which to begin speaking of the various Latinx communities. For instance, Lawrence La Fountain-Stokes, gay Puerto Rican author, literary critic, and performer, notes that when the category of Latina writings is expanded and complicated, it is conceivable that it can include the work of women such as Sor Juana Inés de la Cruz, a Mexican feminist of the seventeenth century. He argues, "The category of Latina/o can be productively challenged, conceptualized, and expanded, whether by virtue of linguistic affinities (the Spanish language), or country of origin (Spain and Mexico), or historical anachronism; queer Latina/o cultural archives include multiple, uncontainable sources."[5] Even when we shift our gaze to the United States, there are multiple possible points of origin. Virginia Sánchez Korrol notes that "the first historical novel ever written in the United States might have been *Jicoténcal*, penned by Cuban Félix Varela in Philadelphia in 1826."[6] The first Spanish-language newspaper, *El Misisipí*, was published in New Orleans in 1808, and it was a New Orleans Latinx newspaper, *La Patria*, that spoke out against the behavior of the United States during the U.S. Invasion of northern Mexico (1846–48).[7] This rich plurality constructed frames from which the fields of Chicanx and Latinx studies emerged; yet that same plurality resulted in diverse approaches to the field, its points of origin, and even its definition.

The term *Latina/Latino/Latinx* can, at times, erase differences. Thus, in our handbook, we are careful to use language to
name specific communities, using *Latinx* for those times when
we are addressing material rooted in our collective knowledges
and/or experiences. To provide a glimpse of Latinx diversity, we
briefly address the origins of the relationship of five of our communities to the United States. The snapshots briefly map U.S.
colonialist relationships to the Americas, and the responses to
these relationships on the part of our diverse communities. We
believe this overview demonstrates that each of our communities
brings a different response to U.S. imperialism, and a different,
rich history, to the building of community in the United States.
It also demonstrates how we have some things in common.

The histories of people of Mexican, Puerto Rican, Cuban,
Salvadoran, and Guatemalan ancestry in relation to the United
States are strikingly varied, and the task of detailing them here
is an impossible one. It is important, however, to consider that
each of these ethnic groups relates to the United States differ-
ently, whether in terms of annexation, migration, diaspora, or
exile.[8] We see this clearly in Chicanx and Puertorriqueñx histories. After pursuing its "Manifest Destiny" and concluding the
war against Mexico in 1848, the United States annexed more
than half of Mexico's territory with the broken promises that
Mexican citizens would keep their land, language, and economic
power. Instead, Mexicans became second-class citizens in a
"new country," in their old land.[9] Before the war, moving north
was a matter of relocating within their own country. After the
war, moving north meant moving into a hostile land that "was
Mexican once" but was now part of the United States.

For Puerto Ricans, the United States represents a totalizing
imperialist power given the island's relationship to this country
as a "free associated state," a euphemism for *colony*.[10] Puerto Rico
became a U.S. territorial possession after 1898, as a result of the
war with Spain. Note how Puerto Rico and the U.S. Southwest

share a complicated history dating to the United States' time of empire and expansion. It is also important to note that out of the five Latinx groups referenced here, Puerto Ricans are the only ones that historically have not been concerned with migrating to the United States as undocumented people.[11] In 1917 its people became second-class U.S. citizens without the right to vote in federal elections.[12] The most important waves of migration to the U.S. mainland, and especially to New York, occurred in the 1920s, 1930s, and 1950s.[13] As Puerto Ricans move to the mainland, they, like Latinx immigrants, face discrimination in education, employment, and day-to-day living.

For the same reason and in the same year as Puerto Rico, Cuba also became a U.S. possession; its colonial status, however, lasted only until 1902, although the colonial relationship of American capital to the country lasted much longer. The first wave of Cuban migration to the United States happened in the late 1860s as Cubans responded to labor demands and migrated to Florida to work in its tobacco fields and cigar factories.[14] The second migration wave (by mostly middle- and upper-class white Cubans) occurred in 1959 when Fidel Castro deposed Fulgencio Batista's dictatorship and imposed a socialist state. Finally, the third important wave of Cuban immigrants was in 1980 when the Marielitos, whom the press and government officials described as the "unwanted homosexuals, and mentally ill of the island," arrived. In reality most immigrants were political refugees, including out LGBTQ people, rejected by their home country.[15]

Like so many Latinx immigrants who came before them, Guatemalan and Salvadoran immigrants came to the United States, in part, due to U.S. intervention in their home countries. Whereas the United States took northern Mexico through the invasion of 1846–48, and Puerto Rico through a war of empire with Spain, U.S. involvement in Central America was primarily political and economic: mainly economic in the nineteenth century, and increasingly political in the twentieth. By the mid-twentieth century,

U.S. government and corporate support of repressive regimes was contributing to ongoing movement within and between El Salvador, Guatemala, and Honduras. An infamous example of this involvement is the 1954 U.S.-sponsored overthrow of the democratically elected president of Guatemala, Jacobo Árbenz Guzmán.[16] Later, from the 1960s to 1977, and again in the 1980s, the U.S. government provided military aid to the Guatemalan military, even while the U.S. State Department reported "kidnapping, torture, and summary execution" by that same military.[17] Similarly, in El Salvador, while government violence and repression targeting peasants, labor organizers, teachers, and catechists increased, the United States increased aid to the government. Under President Ronald Reagan, government military aid to El Salvador increased from $103 million in 1981 to $412.6 million in 1984. Refugees moved within their home countries and beyond their home countries, often first to Mexico and then to the United States.[18] Because the U.S. government supported the violent regimes of El Salvador and Guatemala, it also refused to grant refugee status to people fleeing the violence it supported.[19]

Always Resistance

Although each group's history and relationship to the United States is remarkably different, in general terms, Latinas/os/xs (especially when grouped as such) still maintain a marginalized status in the United States. Because of their subalternity as colonized subjects, Latinx scholars have been able to create contestatory bodies of work challenging dominant narratives which have, in the past, denigrated our communities; we have produced histories, art, and literature that speak to our communities and to the dominant culture, creating and re-creating what it means to be "American."

In this handbook we understand Chicanx/Latinx studies as rooted in "the long history of revolutionary and anti-colonial thought" developed by and acted upon by the Latinx peoples of the Americas. We affirm the work of Ronald Mize, who argued, "'The long history of revolutionary and anti-colonial thought is always already present in Latina/o political consciousness."[20] The roots of the field, then, are found in the anti-imperialist publications of Félix Varela, as well as in the speeches of Cuban author and revolutionary thinker José Martí and in the resistance work of Las Hijas de Cuauhtémoc, who called for revolution and women's rights in early twentieth-century Mexico. This field of study is rooted both in word and in action. As noted by anthropologist Michelle Téllez, our work "both challenges claims of objectivity and links research to community concerns and social change . . . creating bridges between the production of knowledge in the academic world and communities struggling for social change."[21] What follows is a brief overview of the activism that made our academic fields possible as well as a mapping of some of the ways in which our communities—Chicanx, Puerto Rican, Cuban, Central American, South American, and others woven together—make our work possible.

The emergence of our academic fields is rooted in the weaving of our communities' activism in word and action. While in the nineteenth century Félix Varela penned his novel and news editors in Louisiana produced their newspapers, which were read throughout the Americas, our Cuban, Puerto Rican, and Chicanx communities founded mutualistas, culturally grounded mutual aid societies, to support each other. Mutualistas brought communities together to celebrate national holidays, pooled resources for burial insurance, and created opportunities for both men and women to develop leadership skills.[22] On the West Coast they emerged in the late nineteenth century following the U.S. Invasion and the displacement of Mexicans and Mexican Americans from their lands, jobs, and social positions. On the East Coast mutualistas thrived following the influx of Puerto Ricans in the 1910s and 1920s. At times, as with the mutualistas of Texas, the organizations engaged in political work—for example, fighting to end lynching.[23] William D. Carrigan and Clive Webb point out the intersection of the work of Latinx newspapers and mutualistas in trying to end anti-Latinx violence, especially lynching, in Texas; such labor helped build the groundwork for the generation that followed.[24]

When we look to Chicanx activism of the 1930s and '40s we also see the collaboration and coalition of our communities weaving together as they fought for justice. Some historians, such as David Gutiérrez, see this generation as the one that laid the critical groundwork that made the liberation movements of the late twentieth century possible. Amid this activism we see Luisa Moreno, who came to the United States from Guatemala at the age of twenty-two. Working with Chicanx organizers such as Emma Tenayuca and Josefina Fierro de Bright, Moreno advocated for workers' rights, was a critical force behind the first national meeting of the Congress of Spanish-Speaking People, and worked with Bert Corona and Carey McWilliams leading the Sleepy Lagoon Defense Committee in the 1940s. Even after being deported she continued to work for justice first in Mexico, then in Cuba, and finally in her home country of Guatemala.[25]

The activism of the 1960s and '70s, then, built on this long history of resistance; at the same time the '60s and '70s stand out as a time of liberation, reclamation, and new beginnings. In Chicago, following the police shooting of an unarmed teen, the Young Lords, a neighborhood youth organization begun in 1962, grew into the Young Lords Organization (YLO). The YLO published a newspaper, formed coalitions with the Black Panthers, fought urban renewal, and supported Third World liberation movements. This activism quickly spread to Philadelphia and New York.[26] In New York, the branch would become the Young Lords Party, separate from, yet with connections to, the original organization. While some historians, in looking to the past and the founding of organizations such as the Young Lords, point to the time as one of an exclusive nationalism, others point out the "flexibility" of the nationalism of the time. At least one-third of the Young Lords were African American or from a Latinx community other than Puerto Rican.[27] As noted by Johanna Fernández, "non–Puerto Rican members were not merely passive participants in the organization but were integral to its lifeblood.... [Denise] Oliver [an African American] was the first woman elected to the Young Lords' central committee. Pablo Yoruba Guzmán, one of the founders of the New York branch and a member of the central committee was of Afro-Cuban parentage, and Omar López, the primary strategist of the Chicago YLO, was Mexican American."[28]

The leadership of Oliver raises another important issue, and that is the myth of exaggerated sexism within the liberation movements of the time. This is not to say that sexism was not a critical problem in many, if not most, nationalist organizations; rather, it is to say that such sexism was a product of, and reflective of, the dominant society as much as of our own communities. As Mirta Vidal pointed out in a Chicana publication in 1969:

> The submission of women, along with institutions such as the church and the patriarchy, was imported by the European colonizers, and remains to this day part of Anglo society. Machismo—in English, "male chauvinism"—is the one thing, if any, that should be labeled an "Anglo thing."[29]

In both the Puerto Rican and Chicanx liberation movements women fought for voice and power. In the Young Lords they were often successful. Here, historians point to the inclusion of women's rights in the Young Lords' original Thirteen-Point Program and Platform. The original 1969 program and platform included a point which read, "Machismo must be revolutionary and not oppressive." But the women of the Young Lords challenged this, asking, "Can racism be revolutionary and not oppressive?" They argued that both racism and sexism are oppressive ideologies. The next year that point was deleted and a new point was added: "We want equality for women. Down with machismo and male chauvinism."[30]

The Thirteen-Point Program and Platform was revolutionary, reflecting the hope and optimism of the time—that society can change for the better. The Young Lords called for, among other things:

Self-determination for all Latinos
Liberation for all Third World people
True education
Equality for women
A socialist society.[31]

On the West Coast the work of the United Farm Workers took hold. Originally the National Farm Workers Association (NFWA), it focused on tenant rights, building self-help cooperatives (similar to early mutualistas), fighting police brutality, and getting worker's compensation for farmworkers. In 1965, Larry Itliong of the Agricultural Workers Organizing Committee (AWOC) approached César Chávez and Dolores Huerta, asking them to support striking Filipino workers in the Coachella Valley, and from this collaboration a more powerful union was forged. Together the workers from AWOC, the NFWA, and their allies brought farmworkers to the attention of the national public. Through a struggle that lasted five years, they won, for farmworkers throughout the nation, the right to contract.[32]

Overlapping with farmworker activism, in 1969 two critical conferences of activists and scholar-activists demanded education of, for, and by Chicanx communities. The first one was the National Youth Liberation Conference, called by the Crusade for Justice. Founded by Rodolfo (Corky) Gonzales, the Crusade had its own press, legal services, a bilingual school for preschool and elementary school children, and more. The first national conference was attended by over one thousand Chicanxs from throughout the United States, and attendees endorsed El Plan Espiritual de Aztlán, drafted by the poet Alurista, calling for a new understanding of Chicanas/os/xs as a unified people.[33] Its opening statement declared:

> Brotherhood unites us, and love for our brothers makes us a people whose time has come and who struggles against the foreigner "gabacho" who exploits our riches and destroys our culture. With our heart in our hands and our hands in the soil, we declare the independence of our mestizo nation. We are a bronze people with a bronze culture. Before the world, before all of North America, before all our brothers in the bronze continent we are a nation, we are a union of free pueblos, we are Aztlán. Por La Raza todo. Fuera de La Raza nada.[34]

The document, like the Thirteen Points of the YLO, called for revolutionary change including the following:

Economic self-determination
Self-defense
Culture
Political liberation
Education.

While the document had many things in common with the Thirteen Points, including a call for economic self-determination, political liberation, and education, it failed to address machismo in our communities. Unlike the Thirteen Points, El Plan Espiritual was not successfully challenged to include women's equality.

The conference and the plan, however, had a strong influence on a conference of students and educators held in Santa Barbara later that year, and it was there that our communities demanded changes to education in our universities, including a demand and plan of action to found Chicano studies programs. In fact, the subtitle of the Plan de Santa Bárbara was "A Chicano Plan for Higher Education." El Plan de Santa Bárbara mapped how un-

equal educational opportunities and a racist, Eurocentric curriculum contributed to low graduation rates from high schools and
underrepresentation in universities and the professions. Racist
narratives in the public schools and universities created inferiority complexes in students of Mexican descent *and* a false sense of
entitlement among Euro-American students. In order for society to change, universities, along with the other Euro-dominant
institutions of the time, needed to transform. Thus, the Plan de
Santa Bárbara demanded a curriculum designed by Chicanos in
collaboration with our communities, and it included plans for
establishing and growing Chicano studies programs throughout
the United States.[35] Activists, educators, and scholar-activists of
the liberation movements demanded and created a foundation
for the Chicanx, Puerto Rican, and Latinx studies programs that
we have today.

Foundationally, these initial programs were designed primarily by men and centered the heterosexual, male experience, which
motivated Chicana and Latina feminists to transform the field.
Chicanx/Latinx studies, in its present form, owes much to the
work produced in the 1960s during the civil rights and liberation
movements in which people of color reclaimed their rights and
cultures while denouncing their second-class status. Looking to
the field of Latinx theater provides an example and a lens into
some of these connections. The work of ensembles like El Teatro Campesino (ETC) and the Puerto Rican Traveling Theater
(PRTT) brought college students and activists together and made
theater accessible to workers, organizers, and our larger communities. Later, both companies also offered writing and acting
workshops that produced some of the most famous Latina/o actors and playwrights. Unlike ETC, PRTT was run and directed
by Miriam Colón, who addressed women's issues and struggles
within and outside of the ensemble.[36]

El Teatro Nacional de Aztlán (TENAZ), founded in 1971,
demonstrates how the ongoing struggle against sexism birthed a
number of strong Chicana feminist organizations—organizations

that continue to support Chicanas, Latinas, and queer Latinxs in academe and the arts. Formed as a Chicano theater organization to address the racism and inequality of the time, TENAZ had a narrowly conceived nationalist agenda that privileged male power. Eventually women who were members of separate ensembles within TENAZ formed their own organization called Women in Teatro (WIT), facilitating the creation of all-women ensembles in California like Teatro Raíces and Teatro Chicana in San Diego, and Las Cucarachas, led by Dorinda Moreno, in San Francisco.[37] The struggles and lasting contributions of Chicanas and Puertorriqueñas in theater were reproduced in most fields within Chicanx and Latinx studies, where women fought for space in the programs and departments that were founded on university campuses, and for representation in the National Association for Chicano Studies, renamed the National Association for Chicana and Chicano Studies (NACCS) in 1995.[38]

In the 1980s, when Central American refugees arrived in the United States into a world now thriving with Chicanx and Puerto Rican networks and resources, they too built networks, mutual aid societies, and community centers. Salvadoran refugees, U.S. immigration lawyers, and religious and secular activists joined together to found organizations such as CARECEN (Central American Refugee Center) and El Rescate. Centers such as these aided communities with legal counseling, English language and literacy education, and more.[39] Throughout the 1980s and into the 1990s, despite anti-immigration movements, Central American immigrants and refugees were critical to the revitalization and growth of unions in the service sectors of the United States.[40] In relation, veterans of the Chicano Movement became involved in protests and advocacy for and with Central American refugees.[41] Central Americans, by the close of the century, were an integral and critical part of Latinx communities throughout the United States.

Our academic fields emerged out of these weavings, with scholars, activists, and scholar-activists fighting for and establishing Chicano studies on the West Coast, and Boricua scholars, activists, and scholar-activists fighting for and establishing programs on the East Coast.[42] And in 1999, students of the Central American United Student Association at California State University, Northridge, working with faculty including Chicanx studies faculty, successfully fought for the establishment of the first Central American studies minor.[43]

Today, the study of Chicanx and Latinx communities, history, literature, and liberation is more critical than ever. Throughout the United States, between 2000 and 2018, the number of counties where Latinx populations are in the majority increased from thirty-four to sixty-nine.[44] According to the U.S. Census Bureau, as of July 1, 2018, "Hispanics" constituted 18.3 percent of the U.S. population.[45] By 2045 our population will constitute 24.6 percent; almost one out of four citizens and residents of the United States will be Latinx.[46] Colleges and universities throughout the nation have taken note of this trend. Responding to student and community demands, the number of Chicanx and Latinx programs has expanded. While our communities become more numerous and gain political influence, the curriculum in our colleges and universities continues to lag behind student (and faculty) needs. This manual seeks to help close that gap, and with it we hope to inspire you to build upon the work of your antepasadas/antepasados and the workers, scholars, and activists who paved the way for all of us to be here and demand the necessary changes for all of our communities to thrive.

Handbook Organization

We have organized this text into five chapters followed by appendices containing sample student papers and citation guides, and a resource page of scholarly organizations and Latinx and Chicanx online archives. Each of the main chapters ends with discussion questions, to facilitate and encourage student and community engagement. Following this introductory chapter, we address the historical and political roots of labels and self-identifications such as Chicanx, Hispanic, Boricua, and more. If you have never had an opportunity to learn the deep histories behind these names, we encourage you to take the time to read chapter 1.

Chapter 2 is written for students who must learn to research and write history papers. The field has its own chapter because Chicanx and Latinx history courses are among the most common courses offered on college and university campuses. The chapter is detailed: it includes a brief history of our subfields (with a focus on Chicanx and Puerto Rican historians), and a step-by-step guide to crafting a thesis, organizing sources, and drafting and polishing a paper.

As with history, literature and cultural studies classes are among the most commonly offered courses on our campuses; thus, chapter 3 is dedicated to these fields. Here we detail foundational writing concepts like selecting important topics, practicing a close reading of texts, incorporating key ideas into the writing of an essay, and examining the knowledge production of Chicanx and Latinx communities presented through literature and culture.

Regardless of your major, there is a strong possibility that you will find yourself working with oral histories, pláticas, and/or testimonios. You may interview people to learn more about our past, perhaps interviewing family members to learn more about your history in relation to our larger communities. Because of this, chapter 4 is dedicated to working with oral sources including oral histories, interviews, testimonios, and pláticas. Each of these forms has its own set of challenges and benefits; each allows us to amplify voices that might otherwise be silenced by the dominant culture. In this chapter we also address the importance of institutional review boards and tips for approaching the paperwork you should be familiar with as you advance in your studies.

Our last chapter focuses on grammar, language, and structure, offering concise lessons on the use of punctuation, active and passive voice, and sentence syntax, along with an effective set of "Power Writing Rules." We want you, as a beginning writer, to feel comfortable using accessible and empowering language in your history papers, literature essays, and interdisciplinary work. Finally, at the back of the book you will find appendices with guidelines for Chicago citations and a sample student paper using Chicago citations; guidelines for MLA citations and a sample student paper using MLA citations; and a list of useful websites for engaging in Chicanx and Latinx research.

DISCUSSION QUESTIONS

1. What do Noyola's and Anzaldúa's epigraphs inspire Chicanx/Latinx writers to do?
2. Who are the authors of this book and why is this writing manual important to them?
3. What does this book attempt to do and how is it different from other writing handbooks?
4. Who is Irene Isabel Blea and why is her work important for Heidenreich and Urquijo-Ruiz?
5. Why do Chicanx/Latinx students need their/our own writing handbook?
6. What are some of the differences between Cuban immigrant and Puerto Rican histories?
7. What are some of the commonalities that we hold as Latinx people?
8. How do Chicanx/Latinx history, literature, and culture emerge and how do they inform this text?
9. Why are mutualistas and other collaborations among Black, Indigenous, Brown, and other people of color (BIBPOC) throughout history important?
10. Why, for BIBPOC writers/researchers, is it important to "give back to our communities"?

FURTHER READING

Alaniz, Yolanda, and Megan Cornish. *Viva la Raza: A History of Chicano Identity and Resistance*. Seattle: Red Letter Press, 2008.

Anzaldúa, Gloria. *Borderlands / La Frontera: The New Mestiza*. San Francisco: Aunt Lute, 1987.

Capó, Julio, Jr. "Queering Mariel: Mediating Cold War Foreign Policy and U.S. Citizenship Among Cuba's Homosexual Exile Community, 1978–1994." *Journal of American Ethnic History* 29, no. 4 (2010): 78–106. https://doi.org/10.5406/jamerethnhist.29.4.0078.

Chinchilla, Norma, and Nora Hamilton. "Changing Networks and Alliances in a Transnational Context: Salvadoran and Guatemalan Immigrants in Southern California." *Social Justice* 26, no. 3 (1999): 4–26.

Davalos, Karen Mary. "Sin Vergüenza: Chicana Feminist Theorizing." *Feminist Studies* 34, nos. 1–2 (2008): 151–71.

Fernández, Johanna. *The Young Lords: A Radical History*. Chapel Hill: University of North Carolina Press, 2020.

Garcia, Laura E., Sandra M. Gutierrez, and Felicitas Nuñez, eds. *Teatro Chicana: A Collective Memoir and Selected Plays*. Austin: University of Texas Press, 2008.

Gómez, Alma, Cherríe Moraga, and Mariana Roma-Carmona, eds. *Cuentos: Stories by Latinas*. New York: Kitchen Table Press, 1983.

Sánchez Korrol, Virginia. "The Origins and Evolution of Latino History." *OAH Magazine of History* 10, no. 2 (Winter 1996): 5–12.

WEBSITES

Chicana por mi Raza. Archive of oral histories and archival material founded by María Cotera and Linda García Merchant. https://chicanapormiraza.org/.

Latinopia. Collection of Latinx interviews, documents, podcasts, and more. https://latinopia.com.

"Young Lords 13-Point Program and Platform." *Latino Education Network Service*. http://palante.org/YLPProg.html.

CHAPTER 1

We Name Ourselves

Chican@, Latinx, Afrolatina, Boricua, Jotx, Mariposa, y Más

People, listen to what your jotería is saying.

—GLORIA ANZALDÚA, *BORDERLANDS / LA FRONTERA*

Jotería, listen to what your trans* brothers and sisters are saying, and remember those long forgotten.

—FRANCISCO J. GALARTE, *ON TRANS* CHICAN@S*

Desnombrando: Colonialist Origins of Naming

Naming ourselves is a necessary and radical act, for in doing so we claim our identity and exercise the power to declare our intersectionality as members of various ethnic, gender, class, sexual, political, religious, and national groups. Self-naming allows us to claim our histories and aids us in organizing with people from our multiple communities. For all these reasons, and because they grow out of historical experiences, identity labels are powerful. Many early identity labels were/are a product of the colonial era, and part of colonizing processes. As racial projects, they stripped communities of the power to name themselves.[1] Multiple European countries deprived peoples of their culture, their language, their religion, and ultimately their self-empowerment, but for the purposes of this chapter we focus on the Spanish and U.S. colonization of the Americas.

The Spanish empire provides us with an early example of the power of naming. As part of its colonization project, Spain created the casta system, categorizing people in the colonies into more than forty groups according to their ethnic and racial mixing. These groups were a result of racial and ethnic mestizaje throughout the Americas composed of Indigenous, African, Asian, and European (especially Spanish) ancestry. These categories were not neutral; they enabled white Christian Europeans to maintain control and domination over Indigenous and African enslaved communities. Those categorized as españoles were able to join exclusive guilds, hold government offices, and more.[2] The long history of colonialism in the Americas created a caste and class system where each subject was situated in a hierarchical social structure according to their perceived race and/or family background, with white at the top and Black/Indigenous at the bottom.[3] While some categories, especially those in the middle, became fluid with time, the overall structure, where whiteness represented privilege and access to resources, remained.[4] Although by the 1820s many of the colonies had gained their independence from Spain, this system of racial domination and categorization of peoples of Indigenous, African, and later Asian descent remained in place for over a century. Even in the present time, the Americas suffer from what has been termed "colorism," where, among people of color, lighter skin is privileged and associated with high socioeconomic and political status.[5]

When the United States engaged in colonial and neocolonial encounters with Latin America, and with Latinx immigrants and refugees, this type of racism and classism intersected with Northern European and U.S. racism. Latinx individuals and communities responded by creating new identities. These identities are based on their ethnic/racial appearance, their specific time of arrival to the United States, *and* the historical relationship between their home country and the United States. As Chicana scholar and activist Elizabeth "Betita" Martínez argues in her groundbreaking work *De Colores Means All of Us*:

> At the heart of the terminology debate is the historical experience of Raza. Invasion, military occupation and racist control mecha-

nisms all influence the evolution of words describing people who have lived through such trauma. The collective memory of every Latino people includes direct or indirect (neo-)colonialism, primarily by Spain or Portugal and later by the United States.[6]

Martínez's reminder of the trauma caused by new and old colonialisms exerted by various powerful nations is a critical one, especially when she insists that "we cannot understand all that history in terms of victimization: popular resistance is its other face . . . [such as] rejecting the colonized mentality, that pernicious, destructive process of internalizing a belief in the master's superiority and our inferiority."[7]

The Racial Politics of Empire

In the mid-nineteenth century, the U.S. acquisition of Mexico's northern lands brought with it several racial projects: to Coahuila y Tejas (today's state of Texas), it brought a racialized slave system; to California, Nevada, New Mexico, Colorado, and Utah, it brought a belief that God destined Euro-American Protestants to possess the continent; and to the larger territory, it brought legal and social systems structured through a white/nonwhite binary. In 1829, after Mexico gained its independence from Spain (1820), Vicente Ramón Guerrero Saldaña, its second official president and the first of Afro-Indigenous heritage, officially abolished slavery. Yet the northern Mexican state of Coahuila y Tejas remained a slaveholding state. This historical fact is important, as slavery played a central role in Texas's war of independence from Mexico, and eventually in the war between the two neighboring countries. While in 1829 Mexico outlawed human enslavement throughout its territories, Euro-Americans who immigrated to northern Mexico wanted to bring enslaved people with them. In order to maintain their human property, they needed a state that normalized human enslavement through racial categories inscribed in their culture and laws governing marriage, labor, inheritance, and more. The Texas war for independence, followed by the U.S. Invasion of 1846–48, accomplished this goal, establishing a new racial system with Euro-Americans at the top and Indigenous peoples and people of African descent at the bottom.[8] Texas entered the union as a slave state.

By 1848, when the Mexican-American War ended, the United States had taken the territory that belonged to Indigenous peoples first, to Spanish colonialists second, and to Mexican citizens third. This territory measured over 500,000 square miles in size and included the present-day states of California, Nevada, Utah, Arizona, New Mexico, and Texas, as well as over half of Colorado and a portion of Wyoming and Kansas. The newly arrived Euro-Americans erased the history of the land and of the people who had inhabited it. The communities of what had been northern Mexico became racialized foreigners in their own land.[9] The land theft and its legacies inspired the now-famous words of Gloria E. Anzaldúa: "This land was Mexican once, Indian always, and is, and will be again."[10]

Within this newly conquered territory, its various colonized peoples, primarily of Indigenous, Spanish, Mexican, and African ancestry, now found themselves second- or third-class citizens. In an attempt to maintain and gain access to status and resources, many negated their Indigenous and/or African roots. As Pulido and Pastor succinctly note:

> Because the treaty stipulated [Mexican] inclusion as citizens, they legally became white in order not to contravene the United States naturalization laws, which reserved citizenship for whites. But while the treaty may have declared Mexican Americans to be white, they were not treated as such, something that opened up multiple racial paths toward claiming rights. . . . In Texas during World War II, Mexican Americans pressured Texas legislators to pass a bill banning discrimination against members of the Caucasian race—since both the treaty and Texas law certified Mexicans

as Caucasian. Tellingly, the law never passed, and it remained perfectly legal to discriminate against Mexicans.[11]

Following the invasion of northern Mexico, the United States entered the Spanish-American War, taking the lands of Puerto Rico and the Philippines, and attaching the Platt Amendment to the Cuban Constitution declaring its right to intervene in that country.[12] It was an age of militant white supremacy, and the socio-military tools the United States had used to take the lands of Mexico and the Indigenous nations of North America, it now used in its greater wars of imperialism. As observed by Gervasio Luis García, it is not a coincidence that "87 percent of the North American generals who were involved in the guerrilla warfare [in Puerto Rico and the Philippines] had participated in the struggles against the North American Indians."[13] As the Euro-Americans had brought their racial projects to northern Mexico, so they brought them to the Philippines, to Cuba, and to Puerto Rico.

Throughout most of the 1900s, the U.S. government and U.S. businesses intervened in many Latin American countries' political and economic regimes, often establishing and backing right-wing and authoritarian governments. Ronald L. Mize notes,

> Often military dictatorships, bolstered by the US government, were installed to ensure US corporate and anti-communist interests. . . . These dictatorships included Bonilla in Honduras (1912–1913), Trujillo in the Dominican Republic (1930–61), post-Árbenz installed presidents in Guatemala (1954–86), Somoza in Nicaragua (1936–79), and military dictatorships in Argentina, Bolivia, Brazil, Chile, Colombia, Cuba, Ecuador, El Salvador, Panamá, Paraguay, Peru, Uruguay, and Venezuela.[14]

Such interventions spurred the continental migrations of political, economic, and other refugees fleeing poverty and various types of violence, including homophobia and transphobia.[15] The diversity of the refugees coming to the United States was rich in terms of ethnicity, language, politics, and nationality; each community had a unique history and culture. Claiming the right to name themselves/ourselves would require a long struggle.

Umbrella Terms and Government Interventions

The U.S. government endeavored to name these ethnic groups collectively, often through a linguistic or Eurocentric ethnic affinity. Some of the earliest terms were *Latino* and *Hispano*, yet it is unclear if these terms emerged from the top down, from the bottom up, or from somewhere in the middle. According to Ramón A. Gutiérrez, who identifies as a Chicano gay historian, the term "'Latino' is short for *Latino Americano* . . . and it's the result of what happens between 1808 and 1821 as the Latin American countries become independent." He also notes that *Latino* and *Hispano* had been used during the nineteenth century (especially in the second half) in the Southwest, but by 1920 both terms had "virtually disappeared."[16]

The late twentieth century saw increased efforts on the part of the U.S. government to name and shape communities of Latin American descent. During the 1960 campaign for president of the United States, John F. Kennedy's team developed the "Viva Kennedy" campaign to take advantage of his Catholic identity in an effort to unify the Mexican, Puerto Rican, and Cuban vote on his behalf. As a first attempt to join these groups together, it was successful in bringing Kennedy to the White House, yet political support by the diverse Latinx communities did not result in political or socioeconomic support from the newly elected president. Instead, Kennedy broke the promises he had made to them. In the following decade, under the Nixon administration, the term *Hispanic* was mobilized and deployed by the government. As noted by Manuel Pastor, the Nixon administration

sought to create categories for gathering data on the U.S. population, and also "to separate Latinos from African Americans
not just in the data but in the politics of the times."[17] The 1960s
and 1970s had seen strong coalitions among African Americans,
Chicanos, Puerto Ricans, and other communities of color, and
the Nixon administration saw these as a threat.[18] Nixon's mobi-
lization of the term *Hispanic* demonstrates how identity labels
are not politically neutral.

By the 1980s both the U.S. government and marketing firms
had adopted the term, and together they proclaimed the next
ten years as "the Decade of the Hispanic." Television stations
like Univisión and Telemundo capitalized on our population's
economic growth. While their efforts resulted in an increased
acceptance of the term, the term erased differences, much like
the racism of the conquering Euro-Americans during the nineteenth century. Professor of Latin American and Latinx studies
Suzanne Oboler has mapped how the term

> lumps together recent political refugees from El Salvador with
> past political exiles like the first wave of Cubans who arrived in
> the early 1960s. The latter's upper- and middle-class status and ra-
> cial composition in turn masks the differences between their en-
> try process and experiences and those of the nonwhite working-
> class Cuban "Marielitos," for example, who arrived in 1980.[19]

Throughout the 1980s, *Hispanic* remained a contested term. In
addition to erasing socioeconomic and cultural differences, the
label derived from the word *Hispa*, referring specifically to Spain.
Though unifying to some, it was/is insulting and disrespectful to
others who did not privilege their white European ancestry but
instead took pride in their Indigenous and/or other ethnicities
as integral aspects of their identity. The term also made reference to "Spanish-speaking" communities, uniting people from
the Americas (except Brazil, given that Portuguese is its official
language) with people from Spain.

Civil Rights: On Our Own "Terms"

During the era of the civil rights movements, activists of Mexican descent adopted *Chicano* as their preferred name for themselves. While in the past many middle-class Mexican Americans had deployed it as a negative term for working-class Mexican Americans, the activists of the 1960s and 1970s took pride in their working-class roots. As Chicanos (and Chicanas), they named themselves as politically active members of a community with a rich history of resistance to U.S. imperialism and domination. According to Chicano anthropological folklorist José Limón, in print the term *Chicano* dates back to 1911. In that year, *La Crónica*, a Spanish-language newspaper, published jokes and popular anecdotes in which "Chicano" referred to working-class people with little formal education.[20] Arnoldo De León, Richard Griswold del Castillo, and other scholars such as Suzanne Oboler map how the term was appropriated by college and high-school students who were militant in demanding their educational and civil rights as they became active in organizations such as the United Farm Workers.[21] Their activism was part of what today we call the Chicano Movement. Oboler notes:

> Emphasizing the individual and collective empowerment of Mexican Americans . . . Chicano students and youth rejected the assimilationist ideology of past Mexican-American leaders. Instead, they drew inspiration from third world countries' national liberation struggles. . . . The call for Chicano Power, like the institutionalization of Chicano studies, became a significant goal of the movement, as students recognized the need to struggle against the institutions that for so long had made their communities and their histories invisible.[22]

Throughout the era of the liberation movements, the power of self-naming gave rise to multiple Chicanx and Latinx activist organizations. In 1969, in Santa Barbara, student activists created the organization Movimiento Estudiantil Chicano de Aztlán or Chicano Student Movement of Aztlán, best known by its acronym MEChA. Some of these students also belonged to the more militant group called the Brown Berets of Aztlán; Aztlán was recognized as the mythical land of the Aztec or Mexica (pronounced "Meshica") people. Scholar-activist José Ángel Gutiérrez argued that the term *Chicano* derives from *Mexica*.[23] In the United States, the term *Raza* emerged from this same era of activism. It was members of MAYO (the Mexican American Youth Organization) who founded the La Raza Unida Party as a third-party alternative that sought to elect politicians that represented their own communities, especially in central and southern Texas.[24] The term *Raza* (people) generally refers to people of Mexican or Latin American descent who are also politically active in demanding their civil rights. *Raza* or *La Raza* was one of the first umbrella terms chosen by our communities, though it was primarily used by people of Mexican descent.

In New York City, Chicago, and other places in the Midwest, students and community activists of Puerto Rican descent adopted the gender-neutral term *Boricua* (also spelled *Boriqua*) for themselves in order to highlight their Indigeneity and connection to the island's original name of Borinquen or Borinquén. Like the activists of the Chicano Movement, Puerto Rican youth, such as those active in the Young Lords Party, sought to build pride in their communities and revolutionary change in the nation. Because Puerto Rico remained a territory of the United States, the struggle for community empowerment was often tied to both Puerto Rico and the community in the mainland United States.[25]

From the Margins: Chicano-Riqueña and Feminist Collaborations

Even with their different histories, the early 1970s were a time of cross-cultural collaborations between Chicanos and Puerto

Ricans, including in literary studies. One example of this is the creation of *Revista Chicano-Riqueña* or *Chicano-Puerto Rican Review* in 1973, by Nicolás Kanellos and Luis Dávila, out of Indiana University. This journal published poetry, essays, and short fiction by authors like Rudolfo Anaya, Miguel Algarín, and others who had a difficult time publishing their work with mainstream presses. To its credit, *Revista* published Chicana authors such as Sandra Cisneros, Ana Castillo, and Lorna Dee Cervantes, who later became leaders in the world of Chicana/o/x and U.S. literature in general. The Spring 1978 volume was dedicated to "La Mujer" as a special issue—the photo on the cover was entitled *Una Poeta Chilena*.[26] The volume was also a collaboration between Chicana activists/authors and other women activists/writers from countries like El Salvador, Guatemala, Argentina, and Chile, criticizing U.S. military involvements in these and other countries in Latin America.

The feminist issue of *Revista Chicano-Riqueña* was an exception to the nationalist male-centeredness of that time, and, in fact, a response to it. In response to the male-centrism of the movement, Chicanas increasingly demanded the incorporation of the word *Chicana* along with *Chicano*, given the sexism of the Spanish language, which privileges the *o* as (supposedly) inclusive of all genders. It would be a struggle for Chicana and Latina feministas throughout the late twentieth century. For example, the name of one of the leading academic organizations established in 1972, the National Association for Chicano Studies (NACS), did not change its name to the National Association for Chicana and Chicano Studies (NACCS) until 1995. The change was due to the work and struggle of Chicana feminists within the organization.

The term *Latino*, like the term *Chicano*, has a rich history. In the early twentieth century it was used as a coalitional term by Mexican Americans and Puerto Ricans in the barrios of Chicago.[27] Yet it was not until the latter part of the twentieth century that, as a response to the erasure of Indigenous roots by the label *Hispanic*, Latinx communities made use of the term nationally. Later, due to demands from feminists, *Latina* was adopted to challenge the gendered and masculine use of the *o* in *Latino*. Unlike *Hispanic*, the term *Latina/o* represents people of Latin American descent without an emphasis on Spanish as their language of origin; it also includes people from Brazil.[28]

Abriendo Caminos: A/o/@/x/e

The late twentieth century presented continued challenges concerning how we name ourselves. Many scholars and activists voiced concerns about the ways in which *Latina/o* and *Chicana/o* seemed to reinforce a gender binary, where all people stood on one side or the other of the forward slash. Beginning in 1995, in rejection of the gender binary, some began to use the terms *Latin@* and *Chican@* (with their respective plural forms). Chicano trans* scholar Francisco J. Galarte states, "I use Chican@ with the arroba to symbolically gesture a rejection of the imposition and implied male/female binaries of 'Chicana/o.'"[29] Similarly, the much-contested term *Latinx* began to be used in the aughts (the first decade of this century) as inclusive of all genders; some Chicana feminist scholars, however, criticized the use of this term as erasing the work and self-naming of feminists who had demanded the inclusion of the *a* in the name of various organizations. Chicana and Latina feminists faced major struggles to bring the *a* into *Chicano/Latino* and insist that there is still power in the use of the *a* in this manner.[30] Therefore, at times, all three letters are required at the end of these labels: *Chicana/o/x* and *Latina/o/x*. People who object to the term *Latinx* and cite it as "unpronounceable" and as an imposition by English speakers sometimes use the suffix -*e* instead of -*x*, like in the word *Latine*. The suffix -*e* can also be used for any gendered word in Spanish, like *amigue* instead of *amiga/amigo/amigx*.

We must clarify that the majority of these terms tend to be used in privileged, especially academic, spaces and that the public at large primarily prefers terms such as *Hispanic, Latino,* and/or a term that highlights their or their family's Latin American country of origin, at times with the term *American* next to it (with or without a hyphen between the two labels): for instance, one might say, "I am Cuban American," or, "Guatemalan American." Other examples are *Salvadoreña/o/x/e, Venezuelan,* or *Honduran,* accompanied, or not, by the term *American.* In the U.S. Southwest in particular, some community members of Mexican ancestry who were born and raised in the United States have a preference for the term *Mexican* by itself or *Mexican American.*

Betita Told Us So: "De Colores Means All of Us"

As (im)migrant and native Latina/o/x populations grow, in order to reclaim all aspects of their identity, some individuals have begun to recognize their negated or hidden Indigenous, African, and/or Asian ancestry. From the beginning of this century, we encounter terms such as *Afrolatina/o/x* (also *Afro-Latina/o/x* or *Afro Latina/o/x*), to explicitly claim African or Black ancestry along with one's Latinidad (especially in the case of Afro-Caribbean, Central American, and South American Latinxs); *Latinasian* (Asian Latina/o/x), which recognizes the Asian (especially Chinese, Japanese, and/or East Asian ancestry) in the Latinx communities;[31] or *Xicanx*, where the initial *X* signifies a connection to Indigenous roots. Jennie Luna and Gabriel Estrada note how *Xicanx* "reject[s] Mexica-centrism, and instead can be viewed from a broader perspective, one that more widely embraces the Uto-Nahuatl, Mayan, and other Indigenous language families spoken throughout the Americas."[32]

Jotería: Disrupting Binaries

Such resistance and insistence on claiming civil rights has also been the focus of lesbian, gay, bisexual, transgender, questioning, intersex, asexual, and other queer (abbreviated as LGBTQIA+) communities of Latinx descent, especially since the 1970s. Latina and Chicana queer and nonqueer feminists surviving and thriving within academic and activist circles have struggled to have their stories centered, and self-naming is part of this struggle. The effort within NACS to include the word "Chicana" in the organization's name was led by Chicana feminist Antonia Castañeda and Chicana lesbians like Emma Pérez and Deena González, who in the 1980s and 1990s endured violent accusations of being "lesbian terrorists" attempting to destroy the organization.[33] In 1990, the establishment of the NACCS Lesbian Caucus, which was later renamed the Lesbian, BiMujeres, and Trans Caucus to accommodate the needs of its bisexual and genderqueer membership, became a watershed moment for queer Chicanx and Latinx studies in general.[34] Since humor is often an essential aspect of resistance, according to Raúl Coronado, who was the outgoing Joto Caucus representative, in 1993 gay Chicanos opted to initially name their group the National Association of Latino Gay Academics and Activists, or NALGAA (alluding to the word for "butt cheek" in Spanish). Coronado states: "At the 1995 conference the NACCS Coordinating Committee asked us to clarify our acronym . . . they wanted to know if we were an independent organization associated with NACCS." In order to avoid confusion, the name was officially changed to the Joto Caucus in 1995.[35]

Our self-naming and our identities continue to evolve. *Queer* is still widely used by Chicana/o/x and Latina/o/x members of the LGBTQIA+ communities who define themselves as scholars, artists, and/or activists. Yet, while *queer* has strong working-class roots, today it has been reclaimed by predominately white, middle-class communities. Thus, some people of Mexican descent have reclaimed *joto, jota,* and *jotx* instead of *queer*.[36] We also use its derived word, *jotería,* for "queerness." Various urban legends exist about the origin of *joto* (often translated as "faggot") as an insult in Mexican culture, but the first documented instance of its appearance dates back to 1883 or 1885 with the publication of Colombian writer Federico C. Aguilar's *Último Año de Residencia en México.* For Aguilar, *joto* was synonymous with *maricón,* another pejorative term similarly translated as "faggot." More than a century after *Último Año,* in 2007, queer Latina/o/x members of NACCS and Mujeres Activas en Letras y Cambio Social / Women Active in Letters and Social Change (MALCS) collaboratively established the Association for Jotería Arts and Activism Studies (AJAAS), cementing such labels as critical for the identity of these queer Latina/o/x scholars, artists, and activists.[37] As noted by Michael Hames-García, "Jotería studies is not something new. It feels old, continuous with years of organizing, reading, writing, and activism. In another sense, of course, it is new."[38] For years jotas/os/xs have been engaging in jotería studies, reading the works of John Rechy, claiming Sor Juana Inés de la Cruz, and lighting candles to Huehuecoyotl. But in naming jotería studies and bringing scholars together face to face, the founders of AJAAS did something new and powerful.[39] The labor and love of AJAAS continues to call all Raza, all people, to wholeness. Their vision statement stands as a testament to the power of naming and claiming:

A presence of love
Of healing
Of communing among generations
Of solidarity and imagination
Of self-actualization
Where continuous movement of our minds, bodies,
and spirits is encouraged
A world where violence is challenged

Where we voice our pain
Where we heal each other
A world of renewal
A future of abundance
Of transformation
A future where we are autonomous
And free.[40]

As we moved toward the close of the twentieth century, we continued to name ourselves in terms of nationality, gender, and sexuality. Among cisgender and transgender women who identify as Chicanas and/or Latinas, the term *lesbian* is generally associated with white, upper- or middle-class, cisgender women, and, at times, like the activists who reclaimed *joto*, these women draw their identity labels from their own histories and experiences. For instance, Gloria E. Anzaldúa, in her essay "To(o) Queer the Writer—Loca, escritora y chicana," states:

"Lesbian" is a cerebral word . . . representing an English-only dominant culture. . . . I think of lesbians as predominantly white and middle-class women and a segment of women of color who acquired the term through osmosis much the same as Chicanas and Latinas assimilated the word "Hispanic." When a "lesbian" names me the same as her she subsumes me under her category. I am of her group but not as an equal part, not as a whole person—my color erased, my class ignored. *Soy una puta mala* . . . a *tejana tortillera*. . . . Unlike the word "queer," "lesbian" came late into some of our lives.[41]

For Anzaldúa and other Chicana/x and Latina/x queer activist-writers, there is an effort to appropriate terms that were previously derogatory and insulting; in this reclaiming lies the power to name ourselves, rendering those who bully our community with such insults powerless against us.

As we draw our discussion to a close, we draw your attention to the legacies of self-naming that Anzaldúa's generation of feministas left for us. The 1980s saw the publication of three foundational Latina queer/lesbian texts: *This Bridge Called My Back: Writings by Radical Women of Color*, edited by Cherríe Moraga and Gloria E. Anzaldúa; *Compañeras: Latina Lesbians*, edited by Juanita Ramos (Díaz Cotto); and Anzaldúa's *Borderlands / La Frontera: The New Mestiza*. Luz María Umpierre and Anzaldúa are two of the first queer Latina/Chicana authors to be openly queer/erotic and to reappropriate words such as *puta* (whore) and *tortillera* to identify themselves. In 1989, with the publication of the feminist anthology *Three Times a Woman: Chicana Poetry*, Alicia Gaspar de Alba (the only lesbian among the three authors featured in the collection) established herself as a proud "tortillera" with her poem "Making Tortillas":

	Pressed between the palms,
clap-clap	
	thin yellow moons,
clap-clap	
	still moist, heavy still
	from last night's soaking
clap-clap	
	. . . .
	Tortilleras, we are called,
	grinders of maíz, makers, bakers,
	slow lovers of women.[42]

This term remained on the margins, however, until 2003, with the publication of Lourdes Torres and Inmaculada Pertusa's anthology *Tortilleras: Hispanic and U.S. Latina Lesbian Expression*. Torres explains:

> "Tortilleras" in the title of this anthology is one of the many names used for lesbians in Hispanic and Latina contexts. Others

include "jota," "loca," "pata," "marimacho," "culera," "lambiscona," and "pajuelona." Although these words are often used in derogatory ways, Hispanic and Latina lesbians have reappropriated many of them as affirming identity markers. This ongoing project of redefining and reconfiguring same-sex desire has myriad historical and cultural variations that encompass questions of gender, nationality, race, ethnicity, and class.[43]

There are many other terms that have been used as insults and are now "reappropriated" as affirming labels of jotería / queer pride. Yet it is important to note that often the emphasis on such terms lies on butch or masculine-of-center terminology, which in turn marginalizes femme and bisexual individuals within our Latinx queer communities.

One exception to the masculine trend in reclamation is the term *mariposa*, which has been beautifully reclaimed, especially by queer Latino/x men. According to queer Chicano scholar Daniel Enrique Pérez, the word's origin is from the phrase "La Virgen María posa" (the Virgin Mary rests). Pérez also notes how the label "mariposa" references the butterfly as powerful; in Aztec mythology there are several references to this insect's force, including Itzpapalotl—the obsidian (unbreakable) butterfly goddess. Mariposas have become a reclaimed symbol of strength, migration, resilience, survival, and pride. In the words of Daniel Enrique Pérez:

> Those of us who have the privilege of living as visibly queer Chicanos and Latinos can do so thanks to our ancestral warriors, many of whom lost their lives in battle. They assisted in the construction of a Mariposa Nation where others could live freely and safely. Although we still face severe acts of condemnation and persecution, several of us proudly display our colorful wings and are bold enough to venture into inhospitable terrain because we know the value of our presence. With each flutter of our wings, we honor those who no longer fly among us.[44]

By Any Names We Choose: La Lucha Continúa

Regardless of which labels we choose for ourselves, the words of Elizabeth "Betita" Martínez are critical as she reminds us to continue to do antiracist work and to not fall into the trap of letting labels become our primary concern.[45] As Chicana/o/x/e and Latina/o/x/e queers and nonqueers, our work for liberation and upholding our various communities remains at the center of what Gloria E. Anzaldúa calls "work that matters." We must move forward in community and honor the work of our ancestr@s/ancestrxs/ancestres as we face the social, political, and economic challenges of the United States and the world at large.

DISCUSSION QUESTIONS

1. Why is it important for communities of color and LGBTQIA+ people to name ourselves?
2. What is the relationship between naming and colonization?
3. Why is it important to discuss the abolition of slavery in Mexico when we talk about the history of colonization of the U.S. Southwest?
4. What is the origin and the importance of each term: "Hispanic," "Latino," and "Chicano"?
5. How did the liberation movements of the 1960s and '70s influence Chicano and Puerto Rican identities?
6. What are some of the ways in which feminists and LGBTQIA+ individuals asserted their identities within large Chicanx/Latinx organizations?
7. What does Elizabeth "Betita" Martínez state about doing "anti-colonial" work?
8. What are some of the identity labels that you use in your family? Are these the same as the ones you use with your friends?

9. How might the wide variety of identity labels that we have for our communities complicate finding sources for our research projects? How can we meet these challenges?

FURTHER READING

Anzaldúa, Gloria. "To(o) Queer the Writer—Loca, escritora y chicana." In *Living Chicana Theory*, edited by Carla Trujillo, 263–76. Berkeley: Third Woman Press, 1998.

Forbes, Jack D. "The Hispanic Spin: Party Politics and Governmental Manipulation of Ethnic Identity." *Latin American Perspectives* 19, no. 4 (1992): 59–78. https://doi.org/10.1177/0094582X9201900406.

Galarte, Francisco J. "Transgender Chican@ Poetics: Contesting, Interrogating, and Transforming Chicana/o Studies." *Chicana/Latina Studies* 13, no. 2 (Spring 2014): 118–39.

Gutiérrez, Ramón A. "Community, Patriarchy and Individualism: The Politics of Chicano History and the Dream of Equality." *American Quarterly* 45, no. 1 (1993): 44–72. https://doi.org/10.2307/2713052.

Hamilton, Nora, and Norma Stoltz Chinchilla. *Seeking Community in a Global City: Guatemalans and Salvadorans in Los Angeles*. Philadelphia: Temple University Press, 2001.

Martínez, Elizabeth. *De Colores Means All of Us: Latina Views for a Multi-colored Century*. Cambridge, Mass.: South End Press, 1998.

Oboler, Suzanne. *Ethnic Labels, Latino Lives: Identity and the Politics of (Re)presentation in the United States*. Minneapolis: University of Minnesota Press, 1995.

Pérez, Daniel Enrique. "Toward a Mariposa Consciousness: Reimagining Queer Chicano and Latino Identities." *Aztlán* 39, no. 2 (2014): 95–127.

Ramos, Juanita, ed. *Compañeras: Latina Lesbians*. New York: Latina Lesbian History Project, 1987.

Tijerina-Revilla, Anita. "Are All Raza Womyn Queer? An Exploration of Sexual Identities in a Chicana/Latina Student Organization." *NWSA Journal* 21, no. 3 (2009): 46–62. muse.jhu.edu/article/369866.

CHAPTER 2

The Fields of Chicanx and Latinx History

Roots of the Fields

In 1987, the scholar-activist Gloria Evangelina Anzaldúa wrote, "A misinformed people is a subjugated people."[1] Her message, grounded in the rich history and soil of the Texas borderlands, tells us that history matters, for it is a powerful tool that can either support the status quo or challenge it. It can do violence to a people, erasing their past and normalizing their subjugation, or it can liberate, reminding them of their rich and complicated past and aiding them in imagining liberatory futures. As Chicanx and Latinx historians, we are committed to work that contributes to a more just society and that makes our communities stronger. As noted by Chicana historian Emma Pérez, "The historian's political project . . . is to write a history that decolonizes otherness."[2]

Chicanx, Latinx, and other scholars become historians for a variety of reasons. Some of us, concerned with the absence of our histories in the classrooms where we studied as young people, recognize how that contributed to our second-class citizenship in the United States. We want, therefore, to change historical narratives so that future generations of Chicanx and Latinx students can read their histories in their textbooks and discuss them in their classrooms. Other historians are driven by a love of discovering new realities in the archives; still others hope to learn the skill of excavating histories in order to help our communities throughout the hemisphere excavate, document, and pass on our histories. Chicanx and Latinx historians are scholars who want to make a difference in the world and who believe that asking questions about the past can help us do just that. In choosing to learn more about the fields of Chicanx and Latinx history, you are joining a long line of scholars who have used the past to empower our communities and envision a better, more just future.

The roots of Chicanx/Latinx history run deep and are interdisciplinary. Rodolfo Acuña, in mapping the status of Chicanx history at the turn of the twenty-first century, pointed out that it pulls tools from a number of disciplines.[3] Prior to the emergence of the field as a field, George I. Sánchez, Jovita González, Américo Paredes, and Ernesto Galarza all produced work that challenged dominant histories about our communities. Their training was in fields such as folklore, Latin American history, and education. What they held in common was their pride in our communities and in our past. In their work, they demonstrated the power of history to challenge inequality.[4] The field also makes use of theoretical tools such as neo-Marxism, which offer "useful paradigms" for understanding structural inequalities.[5] Likewise, mainland Puerto Rican history, as an academic discipline, emerged out of the interdisciplinary work of Puerto Rican scholars such as Frank Bonilla, co-founder and first director of the Centro de Estudios Puertorriqueños.[6] The scholarship emerging from El Centro was interdisciplinary and revolutionary because "it rejected the traditional approaches to learning about Puerto Ricans and defined new sources of learning . . . it discarded apologist and colonizing ideologies and designed new theoretical constructs."[7]

In this context, it is not surprising that many of our early Chicanx and Latinx histories appeared in community publications and interdisciplinary journals. Enriqueta Vasquez, for example, wrote articles about the history of United States imperialism in relation to Mexico for *El Grito del Norte* as early as 1970, as well as historically grounded critiques of topics as diverse as Spanish colonialism and mestizaje.[8] Her work built on the tradition of Jovita Idar, who throughout the second decade of the twentieth century wrote for *La Crónica, El Progreso, La Prensa,* and *Evolución.*[9] When we shift our gaze to Puerto Rico, the historically grounded feminist work of Luisa Capetillo, whose influence spanned Puerto Rico and the diaspora, can be found as early as 1907 in *Ensayos libertarios.*[10] Over half a century before the emergence of "the feminist movement" in the United States, Capetillo and Idar mapped how the "personal is political."[11]

From their inception as well, our fields crossed borders. Puerto Rican histories as written by Puerto Rican scholars were strongly influenced by diaspora. Chicanx historians were often trained in Latin American history, not U.S. history. As Antonia Castañeda and Deena González have noted, formally trained Chicanx historians of the 1970s and 1980s were either Latin Americanists or trained by Latin Americanists. Thus, early Chicanx histories often noted the complex relationship between the United States, Mexico, and the rest of the Americas. Puerto Rican historians noted the relationship of compatriots on the Island and throughout the diaspora.[12] These relationships remain important, whether we are mapping the critical resistance of Indigenous women to the mission system throughout the Americas or the role of the U.S. government in overthrowing the democratically elected president of Chile in 1973.[13] As Chicanx and Latinx historians we know that the past is complex and seldom contained (if ever) within a discrete location. Instead, the past weaves through space and time like the fabric of a great loom; we seek to map that weave in order to better understand our present and to better our future.

The image and philosophy that the world is woven comes to us from the ancient philosophers of Anáhuac, who understood their world as a great weave, much like the cloth they so valued in their marketplaces. James Maffie, in studying their philosophy, came to believe that they saw themselves involved in this great

weave as actors.[14] The great scholar-activist Gloria E. Anzaldúa
also examined this ancient philosophy and drew our attention
to the manner in which nepantla, for the people of Anáhuac,
represented in-between spaces, spaces of transition.[15] When we
bring these two understandings of this philosophy together, we
can see that for Chicanx and Latinx scholars, especially historians, studying the weave of the past is critical to understanding the present because both tenses are active, woven through
with energy and action, sometimes constructive, other times destructive, still other times both at once. Spaces and times of in-
betweenness wove through the past, just as they weave through
the present. In relation, we play an active role in using the past to
create our present and to imagine and weave tomorrow.

Throughout the 1970s, Puerto Rican and Chicanx historians
excavated our histories, speaking back to the misinformation
found in U.S. history texts, popular culture, and our own communities. Not all of these historians were formally trained in the
academy, and of those who attended universities, not all focused
on the field of history, but each of them shared a commitment
to justice and to our communities. Among the first historically
grounded Chicana feminist publications were Martha Cotera's
*Diosa y Hembra: The History and Heritage of Chicanas in the
United States, Profile on the Mexican-American Woman,* and
The Chicana Feminist.[16] Cotera excavated the activism of Las Hijas de Cuauhtémoc, the Liga Feminista, the Liga Feminil Mexi-
canista, and others who were foremothers of the Chicana activists of her generation.[17] As an elder, she later reflected that her
goal, and that of her generation of Chicana feminist writers, was,
in part, to "uplift Doña Marina (Malinche), the male-maligned
creator of our mestizo race, along with other female leaders of
anti-colonialist battles, all either stereotyped or willfully erased
by social scientists and historians."[18]

Cotera's work was part of a larger gendering of Latinx history.
In 1974 *Aztlán,* which had published very few articles by Chica-

nas, issued Adaljiza Sosa Riddell's "Chicanas and El Movimiento," which traced the roots of sexism to the Spanish conquest; equally important, Sosa Riddell noted how, just as the women of our communities today are not homogeneous, the women of our varied pasts—Spanish, mestiza, and Indigenous women—all had different histories.[19] Finally, in 1977 *Latin American Perspectives*, a mainstream interdisciplinary journal, published María Linda Apodaca's "The Chicana Woman: An Historical Materialist Perspective," which, like many of the Chicana articles published in community publications, contained a strong critique of capitalism. Through her mapping of socioeconomic systems prior to 1846 *and* before 1521, she argued that a gendered and materialist analysis is the key to challenging structural inequalities today. In relation, and equally important, she articulated a theme that continued (and continues) to influence and drive Chicana scholars to do the work at hand: "We must have histories that can be the basis for future social action."[20]

In 1972, a time when Latinx feminist history texts flourished in community publications and had begun appearing in refereed journals, Rodolfo Acuña's now-classic *Occupied America* saw print. Acuña's text was by no means feminist or queer. But his dismantling of the myths of Manifest Destiny and his labeling of the U.S. Invasion for what it was helped historians, Chicanx and non-Chicanx, question how they approached their work. Even his title called readers to examine the nature of "America." Speaking of "occupied America," he argued, called attention to America as a continent of which the United States was a part. The invasion of northern Mexico by Euro-Americans was one part of a larger legacy of imperialism and colonialism in the Americas.[21]

In his opening chapter, he wrote:

The conquerors imposed upon the vanquished their version of what had happened in the wars. They created myths about the invasion. . . . After the conquest, the original inhabitants found themselves continually denigrated by the Anglo-American victors. The fundamental issue that the wars were imperialistic and unjust was forgotten, and the historians clothed the Anglo invasions of Mexican territory with the mantle of legitimacy. In the process, the violence and the aggression have been forgotten, and thus the myth that the United States is a peace-loving nation dedicated to democracy is perpetuated.[22]

In this brief excerpt one can observe many important issues at play. Acuña questioned dominant histories of the U.S. Invasion, and, equally important, he pointed out the role of history and historians in either reinforcing or challenging colonial violence, for, as we established above, history can be either a tool of liberation or of oppression. Throughout his text, he demonstrated how the U.S. Invasion was, in fact, an act of imperialism. Because the 1970s were a time when many historians were still clinging to the myth of objectivity, the reaction of historians to Acuña's work was strong. While some, such as Mario Trinidad García, writing for the *Pacific Historical Review*, praised the long-needed economic analysis of the U.S. Invasion, others, such as Victor Dahl, writing for the *Western Historical Quarterly*, were upset by the tone and berated its "angry statement of charges."[23] Yet Acuña's work was a watershed, and several Chicano history monographs followed. They too would question the mythologies developed by generations of Euro-American colleagues, map the role of historians in creating colonial myths, and bring a fresh, Chicanx lens to America's past.

Most of the monographs that followed were written by Chicano historians and, sadly, like Acuña's early work, lacked a strong gender and sexuality analysis.[24] Yet this rich and diverse heritage made possible the work of later Chicanx historians such as Ramón Gutiérrez, Deena González, and Antonia Castañeda, who, Emma Pérez argues, mapped differences within our communities and gendered our past.[25] In the 1980s a first cohort of Chicana histo-

rians would complete their PhDs in U.S. history. Many of today's
Chicana historians think of this first cohort as "the big four": Deena
González, Emma Pérez, Vicki L. Ruiz, and Antonia Castañeda.[26]
Yet even that first cohort was able to accomplish so much because
of the many scholars and activists who preceded them.

It was not until 1987, with the publication of Vicki L.
Ruiz's *Cannery Women, Cannery Lives*, that we had a Chicana monograph published by a university press.[27] Throughout the 1970s
and 1980s Chicana historians continued to publish and to challenge how we understood the past. They reclaimed historical
and mythical figures that had been used to control Chicanas.
Because distorted histories of Malintzin Tenépal, also called
La Malinche or doña Marina, were so often mobilized to deni-
grate and/or control women, challenging and writing histories of
her life was central to this reclamation. Adelaida R. Del Castillo
led the way with "Malintzin Tenépal: A Preliminary Look into
a New Perspective." In it she argued that significant silences in
the histories of Malintzin Tenépal had given rise to distorted
images of this significant cultural and historical figure. By plac-
ing Malintzin in a larger historical and political context and by
excavating biographical information about her and her family,
Del Castillo made her emerge as "an actual force in the making of
history."[28] Del Castillo's work was followed by Norma Alarcón's
now-classic "Chicana's Feminist Literature: A Re-vision Through
Malintzin / or Malintzin: Putting Flesh Back on the Object" and
Shirlene Soto's "Tres modelos culturales: La Virgen de Guadalupe, la Malinche y la Llorona."[29] As noted by Esquibel, Chicana
lesbians were central to this reclamation and engaged such dis-
courses to challenge the patriarchal structures of their past and
their present.[30]

No historiography of Latinx scholarship, of course, would
be complete without mentioning Gloria E. Anzaldúa's *Borderlands: The New Mestiza*. Writing from a queer mestiza perspective, Anzaldúa's work crossed multiple linguistic and dis-

ciplinary borders. What began as a collection of poetry came to include autoethnography and autoteoría—the study of ourselves and the theory that emerges from reflecting on our own life experiences. Her autoethnography continually zoomed in and out into larger historical contexts as it uprooted and rerooted precolonial and postcolonial stories and histories and challenged traditional ways of knowing the past:

> With the victory of the US forces over the Mexican in the US-Mexican War, *los norteamericanos* pushed the Texas border down 100 miles, from el río Nueces to el río Grande. South Texas ceased to be part of the Mexican state of Tamaulipas.... The border fence that divides the Mexican people was born on February 2, 1848 with the signing of the Treaty of Guadalupe Hidalgo....
>
> ... In the 1950s I saw the land, cut up into thousands of neat rectangles and squares....
>
> To make a living my father became a sharecropper. Rio Farms Incorporated loaned him seed money and living expenses. At harvest time, my father repaid the loan and forked over 40% of the earnings.[31]

As noted by Deena González, "Anzaldúa's negotiation of the muddy waters of history—linking experience, memory, and treaties or wars—signified a new direction in Chicanx studies but also in Chicanx and Latinx history."[32] Today, some of our most exciting work can be found in interdisciplinary collections such as Alvarado, Estrada, and Hernández's *U.S. Central Americans: Reconstructing Memories, Struggles, and Communities of Resistance.*[33] The refusal to claim objectivity, noting the strong connections between the personal, historical, and political, remains central to our vibrant legacy as Latinx historians.

Chicanx and Latinx historians today continue to build on these bold legacies. As we entered the twenty-first century, Teresita Levy excavated Puerto Rican resistance to empire, bringing a fresh perspective to histories of colonialism. Victoria González-Rivera mapped and analyzed women's rights and activism in pre-revolutionary Nicaragua, including the complicated relationship of middle-class feminists to the Somoza regime. Yvette J. Saavedra complicated the way we understand the relationship between land, culture, and social institutions through a deep excavation of Pasadena's history, and in 2018 Dionne Espinoza, María Eugenia Cotera, and Maylei Blackwell published *Chicana Movidas*, bringing together an unprecedented collection of feminista histories from and about the late twentieth century.[34] Espinoza, Cotera, and Blackwell invited readers "to reimagine the archive, its meanings, and our scholarly relation to it."[35] Each new generation builds on the last, bringing fresh new insights into our past and into the many ways we can use it in the present and in the future.

How We Write: "Follow the Sources"

Given this deep and rich heritage, how do we, as Chicanx and Latinx historians, produce knowledge? As noted by Deena J. González in her essay "Gender on the Borderlands," we "follow the sources."[36] But before we approach such texts, as Chicanx and Latinx historians, we ask ourselves several questions. This is because *how* we do our research and *how* we ask our questions are as important as the sources themselves. For us, the *process* of researching and writing history is critical. Here again, the work of Chicana feminist historian Emma Pérez helped build a foundation for our work. It is she who in 1994 wrote, "I am, in a sense, exposing how historians have participated in a politics of historical writing in which erasure—the erasure of race, gender, sexualities, and especially difference—was not intentional, but rather a symptom of the type of narrative emplotment unconsciously chosen by historians. I am wondering what will happen if emplotment becomes a conscious act as we write the events that become our official stories."[37]

What is emplotment? It is the manner in which we arrange the data, facts, and events of our research to tell a story and explain our findings. Too often, Pérez argues, historians arrange their findings into a tidy, linear narrative, where everything falls neatly in line and anything that does not fit must be erased. By insisting on neat lines, the profession of history often played a role in normalizing histories of the dominant culture while further erasing Chicanx, Indigenous, African American, and other critical histories. Thus, even while we search for our treasure trove of data, we must think creatively about how to organize and present it to a wider audience.

When we rush into our work without asking critical questions, we can produce problematic texts without realizing the power of our own words. On the other hand, when we ask ourselves critical questions, reflecting on the power of our words, the history of our field, and the needs of the world around us, we can produce texts that help decolonize the university and strengthen our communities. Here is one process for writing decolonizing, critical histories.

Preliminary Research

Preliminary Research, Basic Steps
1. Choose a topic that matters.
2. Ask, "What is my relationship to this topic?"
3. Read tertiary sources and general overviews; begin a list of search terms.
4. Ask, "What are the gaps and silences?" and, "How can my project contribute to a more just society?"
5. Develop and polish your research question(s).

Step One: Choose a Topic

The fields of Chicanx and Latinx history hold worlds of possibilities for research; therefore, narrowing a field of interest in order to begin a project can be a challenging task. Are you interested in Chicana labor? Immigration from El Salvador? The constitutions of the Dominican Republic? If so, you need to narrow your topic by time frame, by specific events, and/or by region. Sometimes moving to steps two and three can help in this process. If your topic seems too broad, do not panic; as you move through the process of crafting your project, you will also develop your focus. The most critical aspect of step one is that you choose a topic that is important to you and that will enrich your understanding of yourself, your larger communities, and the world in which you live.

If you are having problems deciding your topic, you might look through the index of your textbook, search the databases of your school library, or skim the headlines of Newstaco.com or Latinopia.com. Topics that some Chicanx/Latinx history students have researched in my classes include: *Madrigal v. Quilligan*, the Nuyorican poets of the 1970s, Enriqueta Vasquez and *El Grito del Norte*, the DREAM Act, the National Chicano Moratorium, Elizabeth "Betita" Martínez, Dominicans in Major League Baseball, Justice for Janitors, and the women of the Brown Berets. The possibilities are endless.

Step Two: Ask Yourself, What Is My Relationship to This Topic?

Our social lens always influences our work. As Irene Isabel Blea stressed in the first Chicano research text, even if we are Chicanx or Latinx, we cannot assume we have an uncomplicated relationship with our subject. As people with access to college and/or the university, we may have more privilege than our subject(s); our gender, our sexual orientation, the place where we grew up, and other factors will all affect how we see our subject. If we are conducting oral interviews, these factors will affect how we and our subjects relate to each other. If we return to our hometowns to conduct research, the socialization we have experienced at the university will have transformed us. Thus, taking the time to reflect on our social location and our relationship to our topic is critical. Again, as Blea noted, "good intentions" are not enough.[38]

Step Three: Complete Preliminary Research on the Topic

For Chicanx and Latinx historians, preliminary research includes asking ourselves questions and locating sources that provide us with an overview of what research has been completed and what gaps/silences remain in relation to the topic. Where do we begin this preliminary search? For the most part, it is in what we call tertiary sources, which are not refereed but can provide overviews of topics. Encyclopedias, textbooks, bibliographies, websites, and other reference materials are all tertiary sources. Some of the most useful websites for Chicanx and Latinx history include the following, but keep in mind we have placed an even more expansive list in the appendices of this handbook:

> **Latinopia**. A cultural resource site. Contains some primary material including movement documents/mini-documentaries and interviews with activists. http://latinopia.com/.
>
> **Telling All America's Stories: American Latino Heritage**. Published by the National Park Service, the site has overviews of many broad themes such as immigration, the arts, and religion. https://www.nps.gov/subjects/tellingall americansstories/americanlatinoheritage.htm.

In addition, we strongly recommend contacting your favorite librarian. They often know of many reference sources that no one else has considered. As noted by Neil Gaiman, chair of National Library Week back in 2010, "Google can bring you back . . . 100,000 answers. A librarian can bring you back the right one."[39]

As you read through your tertiary sources, be sure to make a list of the key words you encounter. This will help as you move from your preliminary findings to the body of your research. For example, if you were reading articles on the life of Emma Tenayuca, you might encounter terms such as *Communist Party, Magonistas, pecan shellers, Worker's Alliance,* and *red-baiting.* These are all terms that you could further explore in continuing your research. Keep in mind that different sources and databases often will have various terms for the same topic. You may have already discovered that some tertiary sources have Chicanx and Latinx history categorized under "Hispanic" or "Mexican American" labels. Keeping a list of key terms (and adding to it as you encounter new sources) will help you in developing a rich body of sources from which to work. Finally, after you finish your preliminary research, take a few minutes to summarize your findings in one or two short paragraphs. This will help you narrow your topic and compile a list of research questions when you arrive at step five.

Step Four: Ask the Other Two Questions

Once you have been able to complete some preliminary research, there are two more significant questions to ask yourself:

• What gaps and silences surround and run through this topic?
• How can this project contribute to a more just society and/or make a positive contribution to Chicanx and/or Latinx communities?

Silences are as important as the materials we find in our preliminary research. Emma Pérez built upon the work of Michel Foucault and Chela Sandoval to argue that silences and what we do not find in our sources are as important as what we do find.[40] Similarly, Karen Mary Davalos, a Chicana feminist and anthropologist, wrote, "In the archives or popular culture, Chicana feminists look for . . . silences, and they seek agency in silence. They turn quiet into social analysis."[41] An example of working with silence would be writing about the corridos of the 1940s. Doing so, you might notice that most early twentieth-century corridos do not address women's activism or struggles. A similar silence weighs heavy in the scholarship about early corridos. To turn this silence into action, you must ask questions of it. You might ask yourself: Who was able to write corridos? What were their goals? In the 1940s, in what actions did women participate? When scholars began to study the history of corridos, which scholars were able to complete these studies? Were all their advisors male? Were the scholars all male? Where do we find women's writings from this time? Silences require us to ask many questions of our sources. Listening to silences and seeing gaps means that after reviewing tertiary sources, and before moving further into our research, we must take time out to think about and reflect on the material that we have found in order to formulate questions about the silences we encounter. Often this causes our projects to shift; sometimes our focus shifts to one or several of those silences.

Our second "big question" has to do with community; after reviewing our tertiary sources we should have a strong enough understanding of our project to think about its significance in relation to our communities and the larger society around us. This is when we return to the critical question of how our research will create a more just society and/or empower our communities. If you are researching agricultural workers, how might your research be of assistance to workers today? Children of workers? If you are researching the emergence of Latinx punk music in Los Angeles, how might your project influence and help to empower Latinx youth today? Consciously reflecting on the significance of your project will aid you in maintaining an awareness of the power of your research and your words throughout the project.

Step Five: Formulate or Polish
Your Research Question(s)

Take a second look at your research topic. If you do not already have a research question or questions, this is the time to sit down and draft them. What is it you hope to learn about your topic? In their research manual, Booth, Colomb, and Williams suggest brainstorming questions and then narrowing them down.[42] We too have found this to be a useful process. Either alone or with a colleague, make a list of questions you would like to answer about your topic. Once you have your list, cross out questions that are too broad to answer in a single paper, put parentheses around small questions that will be very simple to answer along the way, and underline the ones that appear to be just right for a college research paper. As you proceed in your research, look for sources that will help you answer the question(s) you have underlined. Making sure to have a solid question or questions before you proceed will help you stay focused throughout the research process and save you time. For example:

> **Original topic:** The United Farm Workers (much too broad).
> **Topic after preliminary research:** Progressive Roman Catholic clergy and the grape strike of 1965.
> **Questions** (note that after brainstorming the smaller questions have parentheses around them— not because they are un-important, but because they can be answered along the way and are not broad enough to be the focus of the paper):
> - What was the relationship of progressive Roman Catholic clergy to the farmworkers of the UFW?
> - (Did some of the clergy grow up in the fields?)
> - What actions did the progressive clergy take during the strike?
> - (Did they go to jail?)
> - (Were their superiors supportive?)

- What effects did the actions of the progressive clergy have on the movement?
- What effects did the movement have on the progressive clergy?

Research and Writing Process at a Glance

1. Follow the sources: tertiary, secondary, primary.
2. Pre-read and organize sources.
3. Take notes.
4. Draft your thesis.
5. Create an outline.
6. Draft your paper.
7. Revise your paper.
8. Give back to the community.

Once you have completed your preliminary research, read background (tertiary) sources, narrowed your topic, asked yourself the three critical questions, and brainstormed research questions, you are ready to begin research in earnest. As with your preliminary research, it will be important to have a game plan in order to be successful in producing a strong paper. Below is one effective method for doing just that.

Step One: Follow the Sources

Here it is critical to keep in mind that there are three basic categories of research materials. Most assignments will require you to use a variety of sources while completing your project.

Tertiary sources. As mentioned above, tertiary sources are a good place to begin background or preliminary research for your project. They draw on a variety of secondary sources, though sometimes a couple of primary sources may have also been utilized. With tertiary sources, it is more difficult to know where the source material came from; it is also important to remember that the essays or articles do not go through an anonymous review. Why use tertiary material at all? Because it can provide a useful overview of a topic, help you narrow your research, and point to silences.

Secondary sources are materials written using primary material. These might be journal articles or books. Refereed works, sometimes called scholarly works, are books and articles that have been sent out for an anonymous review—that is to say, before they were published, they were sent to an expert or two in the field. These persons then critiqued the work to make sure the research was accurate; they may have also sent the publisher recommendations for improving the book or article. The publisher, if they chose to publish the book, would have asked the author to make the improvements before publishing the work. Note that not all books or articles are scholarly or refereed. Because refereed works are more reliable than nonrefereed works, you want to use refereed sources as often as possible.

When consulting a book or an article, always check to see if it was published by a press that sends out its manuscripts for anonymous review. Relatedly, just because someone has used footnotes does not mean that their sources are reliable or accurate. Check to make sure the work is refereed and then read the footnotes carefully. Does the research appear strong to you? Reading through footnotes can seem like an extra step, but doing so may also give you leads to more sources. The *Journal of Chicana/Latina Studies*, *Diálogo*, *Aztlán*, and the *Pacific Historical Review* are good examples of scholarly journals in Latinx and Chicanx studies.

Like tertiary sources, secondary sources reflect the point of view of their authors. Just as your social location, hopes, and dreams influence the questions you bring to your work, so will the social location, goals, and training of any author influence the framing and scholarly production of their work. Therefore, it is important when reading any new source to always ask questions. Returning again to Blea, she insisted that we ask, "Who framed the [research] questions?" and "Who set the priorities?"[43] In addition, as historians today, we ask:

1. Who created this source and what is their background and training?
2. What is the relationship of the author to their subject?
3. What organizations made this work or source possible? In other words, what organization produced the journal? Who owns the press? If grant money made the research possible, who funded the grants?
4. How does this project affect the community about which it was written?

Answering these questions will help you identify the perspective of the author and use their material more effectively.

Primary sources are the raw data that historians use in their work: interviews, historical documents such as diaries, census records, music, newspapers and newsletters, materials found in archives, etc. Any sources written by people who witnessed the event about which you are writing are primary sources, and any source that was available to people at the time of the event may be used as a primary source. If I were researching the history of a barrio in Chicago, for example, I might want to locate a U.S. census for the years of my interest. Studying the census would tell me the occupations of some of the people who lived in the neighborhood, how many children they had, what racial categories the census taker used to categorize them, and more. All this information would have been obtained from a primary source: the U.S. census. Other primary sources might be sheet music from the time, a transcript from a radio show, or a diary.

Today many primary sources can be found in electronic archives. For those of us who completed our undergraduate studies in the 1980s, this seems quite magical. Archives are an important resource for historians because they house entire collections of primary sources. For example, *Palante*, the newspaper of the Young Lords Party, is housed on the site of New York University.[44] Because the site is dedicated to this specific topic, it constitutes an archive. Other archives, such as the Digital National Security Archive, contain thousands of documents, including declassified documents related to U.S. intervention in Cuba, Nicaragua, Guatemala, and more.[45] What brings the documents in that archive together is the role of the United States in shaping/disrupting the government actions of those countries.

Keep in mind that just because a source is primary does not mean it is accurate or unbiased. Anyone observing an event will bring their own bias and perspective to it. Even official documents such as the U.S. census contain biases. Who designed the questions and categories of the census for the year you are investigating? Who collected the data and how was it collected? When we utilize any document, whether primary, secondary, or tertiary, as historians we always approach the source with questions. Relatedly, we try to avoid relying on any one source for evidence. Instead, we muster a variety of sources, seeking to bring them into dialogue with each other.

Step Two: Pre-read, Assess Sources

Once you have accumulated a stack of primary and secondary material, it is best to organize your sources before reading them for evidence and data. To begin, take each secondary source and quickly read through the table of contents, then skim the introduction and conclusion. Doing this will help you identify which scholarly sources will be most useful to you in your research and which sources can be returned to the library without taking a second glance at them. If you skip this step, then halfway through reading a book you may find it is not useful to your current project—even worse, the week before your paper is due you may find you do not have enough relevant sources to successfully complete your project.

As you assess your sources, organize them according to how specific or general they are in relation to your topic. In a sense you began to do this with your preliminary research, because tertiary sources are more general than secondary or primary sources. For example, if my topic is Indigenous women of Northern California during the U.S. Invasion of 1846–48, I might separate my sources into general sources on the U.S. Invasion / U.S. Mexican-War, sources on California during the invasion, sources on the First Peoples of California during the invasion, sources on Indigenous women during the invasion, and so on. The last sources I would examine would be primary materials: interviews, census data, etc. By analyzing primary sources last, I would be able to approach them with the solid background I developed by reading the more general material first—I would be able to read the primary material in context.

Step Three: Take Notes

There is no one correct way to take notes from your sources. Some scholars take notes on legal pads, some on their computers; older scholars sometimes use note cards and code them by topic. I use a legal pad because I can write the page numbers of the source material in the margins of the pages, and when I am finished with a source I can put the material in a file, label it by topic and author, and easily keep track of material for small and large projects. But what works for one author may not work as well for another. As you experiment with different styles of note-taking, it is critical to always do the following:

- Write down the basic bibliographic information of the source (author, title, publisher, and year published).
- Note the page numbers (or paragraph numbers if from a website) from which you are taking the information. This is critical! If you do not carefully note page numbers, when you sit down to write your paper, you will have to return to your

sources to find the page numbers for your citations (which can be *very* frustrating).

• Carefully note any direct quotations you take down. Here the simplest way of doing this is to always place quotation marks around any direct quotation. Once you finish reading a source, do a quick second read of your notes to make sure all quotations are marked as such.

• Have a system for organizing your notes, whether it is by author, topic, or both.

Menchaca, Martha. *Recovering History, Constructing Race: The Indian, Black, and White Roots of Mexican Americans.* **Austin: University of Texas, 2001.**

187. 1824 General Colonization Law, fed. Govt holds all heads of households in Mxc's northern territories (citizens and imm.) eligible for land grants— no racial favoritism—trying to right the racist laws of the past. Yet CA military officers still take the best land.

203. Some political leaders, including MGV in California, argue that newer immigrants/colonist should get less land.

204. 1833 with secularization of the missions, Indians were supposed to be given a town lot and farmland—only after were others supposed to be able to petition for land.

210–14. Reality was that CA governors gave the best land grants to relatives and friends, allies, etc.

217. Post treaty G.H. "Mexicans who were white were given full citizenship, while metizos, Christianized Indians, and afro mestizos came under different racial laws."

Here, note that the complete bibliographic information is at the top of the page. In the following pages, I would simply write the author's name at the top of the page (or the author and book title if using more than one book by the same author). The page numbers from which I retrieved the information are in the left margin, and when I wrote down information word for word from page 217, I was careful to mark the material with quotation marks. These notes would then be filed in a folder titled "Menchaca, Martha."

Step Four: Draft Your Thesis

After completing your research, try to answer your research question(s). This will be your thesis. It may be that there is no clear answer—and then that is your thesis. Take time to review your notes and then draft a paragraph summarizing your answer (do not worry about grammar). Briefly state the answer to the question and name the evidence that pointed to that answer. With this paragraph in hand you are ready to organize your material for the main event.

Step Five: Create an Outline

There are various ways to organize your evidence into an outline or image before you begin to draft the body of your paper. The important thing is that you find a means to organize your data before you start writing. When scholars skip this step, they often find themselves writing a poorly organized paper that is difficult to follow and, as a consequence, is not convincing. One common way of organizing material is simply to list your thesis and supporting evidence in layers, with Roman numerals for the frame of the paper, capital alphabet letters for the smaller pieces/ arguments within each frame, and Arabic numbers for the pieces of evidence for each argument. When I use this system, I think of each piece of my argument as a brick. Together my bricks build the house that is my argument. If one brick is weak, the house will not be stable.

    I.   Thesis and overview: In your opening paragraph you not only state your thesis but provide an overview of the pieces of the argument you will be presenting.

II. Body: While in high school, you may have been told to restrict this to three paragraphs. For college/university courses you will need many more paragraphs to fully support your argument. At times, you will need more than one paragraph to fully map a piece of evidence. Make sure that all pieces/paragraphs support and/or relate back to your central thesis.

    A. Item from overview / piece of evidence to support your argument (brick for house).

    B. New brick.

    C. New brick.

    D. Brick developing large piece of evidence from brick C.

    E. New brick.

III. Conclusion.

By listing the key points of your argument, you ensure that you do not leave out important pieces of evidence. It also aids you in organizing your thoughts. Brick C may need to be moved farther up in the paper to strengthen your argument. Seeing the evidence mapped out on paper helps you build a stronger house. While many historians use the linear outline above, others prefer more creative and/or flexible models.

Step Six: Draft the Paper

Taking the plunge to begin your first draft can be intimidating, but if you followed the steps outlined above, you already have a working draft of your opening paragraph. Remember Step Four: Draft Your Thesis? Pull that paragraph up on your screen, set it next to your outline, and you are ready to begin writing. Read over the paragraph and think about how you can clearly state the significance of what you found. In graduate school this is sometimes called the "so what?" question. Now revise the paragraph so that the significance stands out. Finally, think about how you can provide some context for this thesis. For example, if

I pursued my topic of progressive clergy and the 1965–70 grape strike, I might open the paragraph with:

> The 1960s were a time of activism throughout Chicanx communities. Workers organized in the fields and factories, students walked out of classrooms, and some clergy became involved in these movements. This paper explores the activism of progressive Roman Catholic clergy in the grape strike and boycott of 1965–70. The strike forever changed the way the clergy understood their role as pastors; the ability of the clergy to stand with the people also changed the way many young activists understood the Catholic Church.

Here, note that the opening sentences of the paragraph provide a context for the paper. The thesis follows and is focused on a specific aspect of the movement.

Once your opening paragraph is drafted, it is time to follow your outline and write the body of the paper. Sometimes it helps to take the information from your outline and key it directly into your paper under the opening paragraph. This allows you to write and fill in data as you move along. Some scholars find this method too restrictive and prefer to write with their outline off to the side. The important thing is to make sure your notes and your outline are available for ready use and that you allow your writing to help you think through your evidence. In other words, sometimes as you write, either your outline or your thesis may change—this can be exciting if you "go with it."

Once you have your opening paragraph, begin supporting your thesis with the evidence you found. Here your outline will be important in making sure you do not become overwhelmed by all your data. For each critical point or event that you address in your paper, you will need to provide evidence. In some fields this is called supporting your claims. In the field of history, we speak of supporting your thesis, or subtheses (smaller, related arguments in addition to your main thesis). In supporting all your arguments, you must not only describe the information that you found, but provide footnotes for each piece of information. This is where your notes, if you were careful to include page numbers when note-taking, will make your job easy. Every argument, thesis, and subthesis must have a footnote with at least one source.

As you continue to fill in your outline and draft your paper, keep the following in mind:

- Always have at least one source listed for each paragraph.
- Never over-rely on one source. If you find yourself using one source several times in a row, return to your notes and review what other sources said about this event. Over-reliance on a source not only pushes writers into "summary" mode, it can also result in a narrow or severely biased view of the event.

Step Seven: Revise the Paper

In revising your paper always do the following:

- Review the writing rules in chapter 5: Did you lapse into casual language? Use phrases such as "People have always . . ."? If so, this is the time to edit out that language and replace it with formal and direct language.
- Check for homonyms and subtle grammatical errors. Spell-check will only catch misspelled words. It may not find those times where you used *initial* instead of *interstitial*, or *compliment* instead of *complement*. After you run spell-check, read for errors that your software did not find.
- Remember, your thesis is a house built of multiple bricks. If they are weak, the house will not stand. Make sure all claims/arguments are supported by multiple sources. Again, this is critical. If you find that for two or more paragraphs

you are using a single source, you are probably taking a very narrow view of your topic.

* Make sure all paragraphs have topic sentences and that no paragraphs address more than one key topic. If any of your paragraphs run for more than two-thirds of a page, chances are you need to break the paragraph into two or more micro-arguments.
* Review all quotations to be sure they are blocked or are marked with quotation marks.
* Make sure that your concluding paragraph is consistent with your opening argument. Most of us think and develop our ideas and conclusions as we write. This is part of what makes writing an enjoyable exercise: when we write we learn, discover new ideas, change our minds about important topics. Yet this creates a challenge for students who turn in rough drafts. If your writing experience was wonderfully productive, there is a strong chance that your thesis changed during your writing. Always leave time to compare your opening and closing paragraphs—and to revise your opening paragraph and portions of the body of your paper so that they strongly support your conclusion.
* Read your paper aloud to a roommate or friend. This will help you catch any awkward phrasing missed by your grammar checker. It will also help you hear how convincing (or undeveloped) your argument is.

Step Eight: Give Back

Turning your paper in to your professor is not the last step of completing a research assignment: giving back to the community is. There are many ways that we as historians can give back to the community. Below is a list of possibilities, but you and your colegas can probably think of many more. Sharing our research and using the power of our words is part of what makes the study of history an exciting and powerful practice.

FIGURE 2 Giving back: volunteer to speak at a grammar-school or middle-school class.

- Share copies of your paper with anyone who helped you with the project.
- Use your findings to create a zine (and be sure to distribute it).
- Make a poster of your findings and post it in a public library or school library.

- Volunteer to speak to a grammar-school or middle-school class.
- Share your paper with your grandparents and/or tíos and tías.

Before We Leave—A Note About Archives

Above, we noted that primary sources are often located in electronic archives. Many primary sources, however, are located in physical archives—collections of documents that are housed at a specific physical site, sometimes associated with a school library or a museum. Physical archives tend to be organized in collections that are named after the person who donated them, or, if all the documents are about a single person, the collection might be named for that person. For example, when I was working on a book on Mexican California, one of the collections I studied was the Cayetano Juárez Papers, held at the Bancroft Library, an archive in Berkeley, California (at the University of California, Berkeley). The "papers" included photos, report cards, military documents, and letters. All the documents in the collection were either created by Cayetano Juárez or about him. The Cayetano Juárez Papers were just one of many collections that the archive housed, and I wound up working through several other collections while I was there.

Visiting a physical archive can be intimidating, but also very rewarding. When I first began doing archival research, I found archives intimidating, in part, because everyone else seemed to know what they were doing. After a couple of years working in various archives, I realized that the rules and the procedures for requesting materials are almost exactly alike for most archives. Visiting your campus archives, sometimes called manuscript collections, can help you become familiar with the routine at archives, and you may also find sources there that you did not know your school possessed.

As with the other research tasks, there are several steps to follow to make archival research as productive as possible. Try to visit the website for the archive to prepare for your visit. Unlike libraries, archives do not allow you to remove materials from the site, so plan on staying at the archive while you work. Because the materials in an archive are irreplaceable (one of a kind), people are not allowed to bring pens into the area, only pencils, phones, and laptops. But archivists know that people often come to the archive from class or from work, so most archives have small lockers where you can secure your backpack and any prohibited materials. And archives have at least one archivist to assist researchers. Like librarians, most archivists are eager to help out and tell people about the resources at their site. So, know that your professor and your local archivist are available to help you learn the ropes. With all this in mind, here are some other things to do when completing *archival research*.

1. Before leaving for the archive, take time to review the archive's home page, or "about" page, to learn basic information about the hours they are open, policies, and more. Most archives, including those on college campuses, have shorter hours than libraries.

2. Search the archive's online site and make a list of materials you want to view. Many archives now have fabulous search engines that can find documents by subject and by collection. Each collection has a *finding aid* that provides an overview of the collection, the name of the person who donated the material, and a list of materials available to view. It is helpful to read the finding aid for any collection you use, even if your search finds material from several collections.

3. Once you have located material relevant to your project, jot down basic information/context from the finding aid that each document is part of. This information will be important for you when you begin writing. Keep in mind that for

each document you wish to view, you will need to provide
the archivist with information such as the document name,
the name of the collection it is in, its box and folder number,
and/or perhaps its manuscript number. This detail, however, will not be needed until you request the material at the
archive.

4. As you search the site, make a list of the documents you
   wish to see. If the archive has a request form that you can fill
   out and submit online, this will save you time at the archive
   itself.

5. When you arrive at the archive, you will find a person at the
   front desk, usually right outside of the archive itself. They
   will provide you with a list of guidelines and rules to follow
   while at the archive, direct you to the lockers, and, if you
   forgot to bring a pencil, they may provide you with one. At
   most archives, the person at the front desk is a history fan
   and may want to hear a bit about your research as you sign
   in. At smaller archives, it may be the archivist who signs you
   in. Whether an assistant or the archivist, this person can tell
   you where and how to request your materials. Some archives
   now have computers set up where you can fill out forms
   electronically; others still use hard-copy forms. Whether
   electronic or hard-copy, the workers at the archive can help
   you fill out your forms as you learn the ropes.

6. Take careful notes on all the material you may later use. This
   is critical. With secondary sources, once you start writing
   your draft, you can return to a book if you need to; with
   archival sources, this is seldom possible. Always write down
   the manuscript number as well as the box and folder number, the author's name, and the name of the collection—you
   will need these to cite your sources in your paper. As with
   any other source, be sure to use quotation marks with all
   quoted material.

7. Enjoy the paper chase. Working at archives, you never
know what you may find. Once, when I was at an archive in
California, a colleague called me over to her table; she was
visibly excited. When I asked her what was up, she told me
she had found an oral history of Isadora Filomena Solano, an
Indigenous woman who was central to the history I was researching. For some reason, the history had been placed in a
miscellaneous file. She gave me the manuscript, file, and box
numbers so that I could call it up as soon as she was finished
with the folder. That was one good day at the archive.

DISCUSSION QUESTIONS

1. Why is the work of Gloria E. Anzaldúa important to understanding Chicana
    history?
2. How was the work of Rodolfo Acuña a watershed in writing about our past?
3. What do we mean by *interdisciplinary*? In what ways was the early work of
    Chicanx and Latinx historians interdisciplinary?
4. What are some of the similarities between the beginnings of Puerto Rican
    history and of Chicanx history in the United States?
5. What does it mean to "decolonize otherness"?
6. What is *historical emplotment* and why does it matter?
7. Do you have a favorite method for taking notes from your sources? If not,
    what system sounds like it might work for you?
8. As Chicanx and Latinx historians, what are the questions we ask ourselves
    before we begin our quest for sources?
9. Why is it important to always utilize multiple sources when writing about a
    specific event?
10. After you complete the first draft of a research paper, what should you
    always do?
11. What are ways in which Chicanx and Latinx historians can share our work
    with our communities?

FURTHER READING

Alvarado, Karina O., Alicia I. Estrada, and Ester E. Hernández. *U.S. Central Americans: Reconstructing Memories, Struggles, and Communities of Resistance.* Tucson: University of Arizona Press, 2017.

Apodaca, Linda María. "The Chicana Woman: An Historical Materialist Perspective." *Latin American Perspectives* 4, no. 1/2 (Spring 1977): 70–89.

Castañeda, Antonia I. "Engendering the History of Alta California, 1769–1848: Gender, Sexuality, and the Family." *California History* 76, no. 2/3 (1997): 230–59.

Espinoza, Dionne, María Eugenia Cotera, and Maylei Blackwell, eds. *Chicana Movidas: New Narratives of Activism and Feminism in the Movement Era.* Austin: University of Texas Press, 2018.

Fernández, Johanna. *The Young Lords: A Radical History.* Chapel Hill: University of North Carolina Press, 2020.

García, Alma M., ed. *Chicana Feminist Thought: The Basic Historical Writings.* New York: Routledge, 1997.

Lazu, Jacqueline. "The Chicago Young Lords: (Re)constructing Knowledge and Revolution." *Centro Journal* 25, no. 2 (2013): 28–59.

Pérez, Emma. "Queering the Borderlands: The Challenges of Excavating the Invisible and Unheard." *Frontiers: A Journal of Women Studies* 24, no. 2/3 (2003): 122–31.

Rodríguez, Ana Patricia. "Becoming 'Wachintonians': Salvadorans in the Washington, D.C., Metropolitan Area." *Washington History* 28, no. 2 (2016): 3–12.

Ruiz, Vicki. *Cannery Women, Cannery Lives: Mexican Women, Unionization, and the California Food Processing Industry, 1930–1950.* Albuquerque: University of New Mexico Press, 1987.

CHAPTER 3

The Fields of Chicanx and Latinx Literature and Culture

Roots of the Fields

Chicanx and Latinx cultural and literary critics do not agree on when the Chicana/o/e/x and Latina/o/e/x literary canon begins or whom to include in it. Thus, establishing its origins and param eters is a daunting task. For example, some believe that we can claim the work of Juana Inés de Asbaje y Ramírez de Santillana, best known as Sor Juana Inés de la Cruz, who was born in Mexico in 1651 and produced protofeminist literary and scientific writings until her death in 1695; others claim the controversial, cross-dressing seventeenth-century conquistadora Catalina de Erauso, known as La Monja Alférez (the Lieutenant Nun); still others insist that we must incorporate the work of Inca, Maya, Aztec, and other Indigenous writers and cultural figures, including ones from the Caribbean islands, who created their work during pre-Columbian times as well as during the conquest. An example of the latter is the way in which Chicana feminists reclaim Malintzin Tenépal or "La Malinche." As countries throughout the Americas experienced colonialism and obtained their independence, there were innumerable writers and cultural figures, primarily criollo or mestizo men and a few women, recognized for their written and performative work. Regardless of the point of departure and whom we incorporate into the canon, it is indisputable that this canon contains a rich literary and cultural history, and detailing it here is impossible. Thus, I offer a brief summary and some general themes that established these fields of study.

One of the pioneer scholars of Chicano, Latino, and Latin American literatures was Mexican/Chicano author Luis Leal (1907–2010), who in 1973 published the article "A Historical Perspective," in which he created a chronology of Chicano literature; he sought to mark and establish its deep roots from its incipiency to the early 1970s. Leal divided these literary works into five periods: the Hispanic period (to 1821), the Mexican period (1821–48), the transition period (1848–1910), the interaction period (1910–40), and the Chicano period (1943–present or 1973) ("Historical Perspective" 18–25). In "The Problem of Identifying Chicano Literature," a companion essay he published in 1979, Leal argues that "the identification of Chicano literature has progressed from the narrow, sociological definition to the broad, humanistic, and universal approach. Chicano literature, by lifting the regional to a universal level, has emerged from the barrio to take its place alongside the literatures of the world" (32). A similar argument regarding the move from "the regional to a universal level" can be made for Latina/o/e/x literature from Puerto Rican, Cuban, Dominican, Central American, and South American authors. As will be discussed below, collaborations between Latinx writers and across communities, such as *Revista Chicano-Riqueña* and the Recovery Project, demonstrated the need for creating and excavating their rich cultural and literary heritage.[1]

These literary recovery efforts contributed to the current universality achieved by Chicanx and Latinx literature and culture, which continues to engage with recent political and civil rights movements. Activists define the summer of 2019 as the "Summer of Reckoning," when, thanks to the efforts of groups like Black Lives Matter and many other Black, Brown, Indigenous, and other people of color (BBIPOC) activists, the United States had to admit its centuries-old racism and the discriminatory practices that permeate every aspect of U.S. society. As scholar-activists, we know that the national literary and cultural canons have also been affected by such discrimination. This activism, therefore, has forced the publishing world to fund the publication and representation of narratives and stories from more people of color. We must recognize that these communities have been writing and representing their own lives for over a century in the United States, and even longer when we consider the rest of the Americas (Castañeda and Lomas xii).

In spite of these recent efforts, however, Chicanx and Latinx literary and cultural productions are still underrepresented in mainstream publications and cultural productions as well as in university classrooms. Given this marginalization, and often complete erasure, Chicanx and Latinx authors and artists address topics of self and community representations that highlight their empowerment and, at the same time, contest the stereotypical and racist depictions created by mainstream Anglo-European culture. Issues such as identity formation and racial, ethnic, class, sexual, and gender discrimination are central in much of this work. Scholars focus on the lives of Chicanx and Latinx authors and artists who consistently inhabit a liminal cultural space, or what Gloria E. Anzaldúa has termed "nepantla."[2]

The Chicano, feminist, and other civil rights movements of the 1960s and 1970s propelled many communities of color to produce their own histories and stories in order to have them integrated into college and university curricula, and, in some cases, into high-school courses. The collaborations between Chicanx and Latinx activists resulted in the first literary journals such as *Revista Chicano-Riqueña* (mentioned in chapter 1). Nicolás Kanellos, a principal actor in this collaboration, later established the Recovering the U.S. Hispanic Literary Project, whose many collaborators unearthed some jewels of the Chicanx and Latinx literary canon. Examples are Rosaura Sánchez and Beatrice Pita's edition of *The Squatter and the Don* (1885) and *Who Would*

Have Thought It? (1872), written by María Amparo Ruiz de Burton, a landed Californiana, and J. Bret Maney and Cristina Pérez Jiménez's edition of Guillermo Cotto Thorner's *Manhattan Tropics / Trópico en Manhattan* (1951).

Latino literary and cultural critic Frederick Luis Aldama establishes that, depending on how we select what is Latina/o/e/x literature and who is incorporated into the canon, one can include authors like Nicaraguan poet Salomón de la Selva (1893–1959), who published the first collection of poetry in English by a Central American writer, *Tropical Town and Other Poems*, in 1918. De la Selva, Cuban author José Martí (1853–95), and Dominican writer Alejandro Angulo Guridi (1823–1906) all published in Spanish about their compatriots' lives while they were living in the United States (Aldama 19). Aldama also states that although early novels like Ruiz de Burton's were written for a more rural audience, as Chicanx and Latinx communities became more urban beginning in the 1970s, writers like Oscar "Zeta" Acosta, a Chicano from California, as well as some of the famous Nuyorican poets and other writers, wrote about their experiences for urban audiences (7).

Throughout the 1960s and 1970s, heterosexual, male Chicano authors occupied center stage in the beginning of this literary and cultural renaissance. As Ramón A. Gutiérrez asserts, given that Chicanos confronted "social emasculation and cultural negation," they went

> seeking strength and inspiration in a heroic Aztec past, [which] emphasized the virility of warriors and the exercise of brute force. Young Chicano men, a largely powerless group, invested themselves with images of power—a symbolic inversion commonly found in the fantasies of powerless men worldwide, a gendered vision that rarely extends to women. (45–46)

Such androcentric approaches to Chicano, and by extension Latino, cultures did not create a safe space for women and queer authors who challenged machismo and homophobia in their communities. Early scholars of this emerging field listed Américo Paredes, Mario Suárez, Ernesto Galarza, Miguel Méndez, Tomás Rivera, Rolando Hinojosa-Smith, playwright and filmmaker Luis Valdez, poet Alurista, and Rudolfo Anaya as the "fathers" of Chicano letters. On the East Coast, Piri Thomas (of Puerto Rican and Cuban ancestry) and Puerto Rican writers like Miguel Algarín, Miguel Piñero, and Pedro Pietri (founders of the Nuyorican Poets Café) were among the first recognized Latino authors.

Yet women also wrote and produced works that are now acknowledged as foundational. Again we turn to the historiography of Gutiérrez, who cites the work of various Chicana feminists (both heterosexual and queer) who confronted the masculinist cultural movement. He highlights several examples from the book *Essays on La Mujer*, co-edited by Rosaura Sánchez and Rosa Martínez Cruz (1977), which made important contributions to our field: ten articles that contextualize Chicana lives, labor, family, health, Indigenous ancestors, and other topics that cover the colonial period (1519–1821), the nineteenth century (1821–1910), and the contemporary period (1910–76). Furthermore, when emphasizing the homophobia present in the Chicano Movement, Gutiérrez asserts that in the 1960s,

> Chicanos refused to acknowledge [John] Rechy as a Chicano or even to accept his novels as Chicano literature. Though his mother was a [M]exicana and had raised him in the barrios of El Paso, it was his Scottish father who had given him a name and abandoned him and his mother. It was his name, his homosexuality, and the themes he explored in print that excluded him from the community of young men defined as Chicano. (62)

Chicano and other Latino nationalisms, androcentrism, and homophobia are challenged by the collaborations and publications of many queer and feminist projects beginning in the late 1970s. Other Chicano gay authors like Arturo Islas and Richard

Rodriguez become recognized as queer, either posthumously, in the case of the former, or, in the case of the latter, decades into his career in 1993. In 1991, Chicano gay sociologist Tomás Almaguer published his influential article "Chicano Men: A Cartography of Homosexual Identity and Behavior" and became the first scholar to examine the sexual behavior of Chicano men from an ethno-racial perspective.

The flourishing of Latinx and Chicanx publications was made possible in part by the groundbreaking founding of Chicanx and Latinx publishing houses. During the 1970s and 1980s our communities experienced the creation of a number of Chicano and Latino presses such as Bilingual Review, Cinco Puntos, Tonatiuh-Quinto Sol or TQS, Arte Público, Floricanto, and Lalo Press. These publishing houses, however, printed primarily male, heterosexual authors; therefore, Chicana and Latina writers created their own independent presses to produce their own works. Lorna Dee Cervantes founded Mango Publications in 1976, which was the first press to publish the work of Sandra Cisneros. In 1979, Norma Alarcón founded Third Woman Press. The year 1987 was key for Alarcón's press because it published Sandra Cisneros's *My Wicked Wicked Ways* as well as Luz María Umpierre's *The Margarita Poems*. A year prior, Ana Castillo published her second chapbook, *The Invitation* (Gaspar de Alba 465). These three writers became foundational for Chicana/Latina feminism and queer letters. As an "out" lesbian, Umpierre established a foundation for erotic Latina poetry and for "homocriticism," or what literary critic Sandra Soto calls "reading like a queer."

Throughout the 1980s, queer poets and playwrights created new work and new spaces. Chicano author and educator Francisco X. Alarcón formed a gay poets' collective called Las Cuatro Espinas with fellow gay poets Juan Pablo Gutiérrez and Rodrigo Reyes; together, in 1985, they published the first gay Latino poetry book, *Ya Vas Carnal*. Francisco Alarcón also published several solo poetry collections in English, Spanish, and Nahuatl. In the genres of drama and performance, Chicano authors Luis Alfaro and Ricardo Bracho and Cuban American playwright Eduardo Machado were prolific. Alfaro and Bracho studied with maestra María Irene Fornés, who, throughout the late twentieth century, mentored the majority of the Latina/o/e/x authors in theater and performance. Queer Latinx novels also began to emerge. In addition to Arturo Islas and John Rechy, in 1988 Cuban American gay author Elías Miguel Muñoz published *Crazy Love*—a novel about the strict family life and tragic violence suffered by a young gay protagonist as a result of Cuban machismo. Aldama argues that during this time, "gay Latino literature did not experience the exponential growth of Latina feminist and lesbian literature and its concomitant interpretative frames. It was a moment when Latinas of all different cultural traditions and ancestry were reaching across tables to find common ground" (101). Michael Hames-García and Ernesto Javier Martínez, in the introduction to their anthology *Gay Latino Studies: A Critical Reader*, argue that there has always been work produced by gay Latino men, but that more archival research must be done to unearth this community's nontraditional cultural legacies. Additionally, they state, "We claim a lesbian feminist legacy of writing as ours in the sense that many gay Latino men have not only found political company in such a legacy, but have found it to be life-sustaining" (Hames-García and Martínez 2).

In order to explore the ways in which Chicana and Latina feminist authors were boldly establishing a critical part of the canon, we must look at the three decades preceding the feminist and queer literary and cultural movements. From the late 1970s into the mid-1990s, Chicana and Latina writers, playwrights, and performance artists transgressed, and continued to question and defy, the patriarchal roles that both the dominant society and their own communities assigned to them.[3] As noted by Chicana queer literary scholar Alicia Arrizón:

[The Latina] subject is the one who replaces whispers with shouts and obedience with determination. In challenging her assigned position, she begins to transform and transcend it. . . . She is the . . . taboo breaker. She is the transgressive, the lusty and comical performer, the queerest among us. . . . Latinas today bring a rebellious sensibility to the task of dismantling the structures that have defined, silenced, and marginalized them. (xvi)

Chicana and Latina writers produced empowering literary and cultural works, and their characters and their own lives challenged boundaries, creating new possibilities for Chicanas, Chicanos, Latinas, and Latinos of their cohort as well as subsequent generations. During the 1980s, these feminists established foundations on which we continue to build today; they created the term *women of color* and cemented the fields of Chicana/Latina feminist, lesbian, and queer studies. Of particular importance is *This Bridge Called My Back: Writings by Radical Women of Color* (1981), edited by Cherríe Moraga and Gloria Anzaldúa (1942–2004). *This Bridge* challenged Anglo-Eurocentric feminism's "global sisterhood" idea and offered a multiplicity of creative, testimonial, and theoretical narratives by women of color (Native American, Chicana, Latina, Black, and Asian) who presented their intersectionality (race/ethnicity, class, gender, and sexuality) as the indivisible driving force of their feminism and coalition building. To date, *This Bridge* is one of the most cited anthologies of its kind.[4]

In 1986, Moraga published her first play, *Giving Up the Ghost: Teatro in Two Acts* (1987), in which she explored the relationship between a Chicana lesbian, Marisa/Corky, and a heterosexual Mexican woman, Amalia. Ana Castillo states that given the fact that her own book *The Mixquiahuala Letters* and *Giving Up the Ghost* were published at the same time, "we [the two authors] read for about a year together, and both of those books interplayed very effectively with each other. We defined them as two stories of two women who find it impossible to love each other in the world of men" ("Interview" 128). Castillo's and Moraga's collaborative work in producing these classic texts is a reminder that writing is a collective project. We do our best work when we remind ourselves that we come from community and we write to, with, and for our communities.

The year 1987 became critical for two additional historic publications in Latina queer/lesbian writings: Anzaldúa's *Borderlands / La Frontera: The New Mestiza* and *Compañeras: Latina Lesbians*, edited by Juanita Ramos (Díaz Cotto). *Borderlands*, *This Bridge*, and subsequent, similar anthologies were published by small, independent presses such as Persephone Press, Kitchen Table: Women of Color Press, Third Woman Press, and Aunt Lute Books. *Borderlands / La Frontera* continues to be one of Anzaldúa's primary contributions to the fields of Chicanx, Latinx, queer, transnational, border, and feminist studies because it established the groundwork for cultural and theoretical concepts related to ethnic, linguistic, and sexual identity and the formation of the people of "El Mundo Zurdo" (the left-handed world), who inhabit physical, emotional, sexual, psychological, and spiritual borderlands. Used in Chicanx and Latinx studies classrooms, as well as literature, philosophy, and history courses, the text is a foundational work of intersectional and interdisciplinary queer feminist scholarship.[5]

Compañeras: Latina Lesbians, considered the first anthology of Latina lesbian voices, assembles artistic and personal stories and creative works by queer Latinas from the United States and eleven Latin American countries. Ramos, a Black Puerto Rican feminist lesbian activist, explains that "with *Compañeras* we are helping to break the silence kept about our lives. We are telling people that we exist. No matter how many attempts are made to deny our existence, to incarcerate us in mental or penal institutions, to rape and beat us into changing, to ostracize us before other women and alienate us from ourselves—we continue to survive and struggle against oppression" (xiii). Tatiana de la tierra (1961–2012), a bilingual Latina poet and activist originally from Colombia, describes the serendipitous inclusion of her work in this book: "I stayed with [Juanita] practically a month. At that time, she was working on *Compañeras*. I remember she had a manuscript, and I grabbed it and started jumping up and down on the couch."[6] De la tierra continues: "I wrote some poem, and she included it in the anthology" (Castro 264). Years later, de la tierra became a powerful author in Latina lesbian poetry; she is best known for her book *For the Hard Ones: A Lesbian Phenomenology / Para las duras: Una fenomenología lesbiana*.

The publications that followed *Bridge* and *Compañeras* brought together many of the feminist and queer Chicana and Latina narratives of the time. Almost a decade after *Bridge*, Anzaldúa's publisher, Aunt Lute Books, publicized her new title *Making Face, Making Soul / Haciendo Caras: Creative and Critical Perspectives by Women of Color*, which compiled the work of seventy women-of-color thinkers, not all of them queer. This book is considered a continuation of *Bridge*. In a similar manner, Carla Trujillo continued and expanded the work of *Compañeras* with *Chicana Lesbians: The Girls Our Mothers Warned Us About*, collecting the poetry, narrative, and artwork of twenty-five Chicana lesbians.

For many Latinas it is Sandra Cisneros's *The House on Mango Street* (1983), Isabel Allende's *La casa de los espíritus* (1982), translated as *The House of the Spirits* (1985), or Helena María Viramontes's *The Moths and Other Stories* (1995) where they first see themselves and their families reflected back from the pages of a published book. Both Allende and Viramontes are known for their works containing aspects of the Latin American literary genre called magical realism. Feminist fiction by Latinas from throughout the Americas continues to grow: Dominican American writer Julia Alvarez's most famous novel, *In the Time of the Butterflies* (1994), about four sisters living under the cruel dictatorship of Rafael Trujillo, became a famous feature film in

2001. Cristina García, of Guatemalan and Cuban descent, published *Dreaming in Cuban* in 1992, and it became a finalist for the National Book Award. These are just a few of the most famous contemporary Latina feminist authors who represent their communities through various sociohistorical and political lenses in their novels. Since the beginning of this century, the fields of Chicanx and Latinx speculative fiction, science fiction, and fantasy have seen the publication of various books, anthologies of new literary works, and collections of critical works. Some examples are Rosaura Sánchez and Beatrice Pita's *Lunar Braceros 2125–2148* (2009) and its sequel *Keep Me Posted: Logins from Tomorrow* (2020), which explore racism and labor exploitation of Chicanx communities in space; and the co-edited volume by Cathryn Josefina Merla-Watson and B. V. Olguín, *Altermundos: Latin@ Speculative Literature, Film and Popular Culture* (2017), which offers Latinx and queer alternatives to the white, heteronormative field of sci-fi literature. Taking a cue from Afrofuturism, Matthew David Goodwin's edited collection of stories and poetry *Latinx Rising: An Anthology of Science Fiction and Fantasy* (2020) compiles the works of luminaries such as Cuban American author Carmen Maria Machado, Nuyorican artist Adál Maldonado, and Dominican American author Junot Díaz, among many others.

As our communities in the United States continue to grow and to speak back, new voices and narratives bring complexity and fresh perspectives to our fields. In addition to speculative fiction, this new century has also seen a rise in Central American literary and cultural works—for example, the anthology *The Wandering Song: Central American Writings in the United States* (2017), co-edited by renowned authors Leticia Hernández Linares, Rubén Martínez, and Héctor Tobar. *Wandering Song* offers the first comprehensive literary collection of Central American short stories, poetry, essays, and creative nonfiction.

The Emergence of Chicanx/Latinx Literary Criticism

By the end of the twentieth century, Chicana and Latina feminist and queer writings were so robust that they gave birth to a new field: Chicanx and Latinx theoretical and literary criticism. Literary critics brought new tools to the fields of Chicanx and Latinx literature. In 1991, Chicana author and historian Emma Pérez established her theoretical concept of "un sitio y una lengua" as she argued that "our works emerge from *un sitio y una lengua* (a specific space and language) that rejects colonial ideology and the byproducts of colonialism and capitalist patriarchy—sexism, racism, homophobia" (161). Chicanx and Latinx literary criticism, like the texts it critiques, creates such spaces. In 1989, Asunción Horno-Delgado, Eliana Ortega, Nina M. Scott, and Nancy Saporta-Sternbach published *Breaking Boundaries: Latina Writing and Critical Readings.* In their introduction, they state, "We focus on an already extensive and rich body of literature written by Latina women, yet virtually unrecognized by institutions of power" (Horno-Delgado et al. xi). Anthologies such as this one helped establish Chicana and Latina letters in academic institutions that refused to acknowledge their writings and fame.

In 1993, Tey Diana Rebolledo and Eliana S. Rivero co-edited *Infinite Divisions: An Anthology of Chicana Literature,* which collects, frames, and critiques the works of more than fifty authors. Two years later, Rebolledo published *Women Singing in the Snow: A Cultural Analysis of Chicana Literature,* where she theorizes the ways in which Chicanas survive in, thrive in, and transgress into traditional male cultural spaces. Rebolledo exalts women she calls "*mujeres andariegas, mujeres callejeras,*" and explains that whenever women step outside of the oppressive roles traditionally assigned to them, patriarchal society considers them lost or immoral women.[7] The author reclaims and re-empowers such terms when she offers the following definition:

> Women who wander and roam, women who walk around, women
> who journey: the terms imply restlessness, wickedness. They are
> not bound by societally constructed morals, nor cultural practices.
> The negative cultural stereotypes placed on mujeres andariegas
> result from a patriarchal culture that wills women to be passive,
> self-denying, and nurturing to others. And [these] women . . . can
> be demanding, self-satisfying, and worse, perhaps they don't need
> a man. . . . [They are] symbols of empowering the body, sexuality,
> and the self. (Rebolledo 183)

Such terms then, can be applied to Chicanx/Latinx feminist and queer writers as they empower themselves by breaking the chains of patriarchy, even at the risk of being considered traitors to their communities and ethnic groups, in order to fully reclaim their experiences, their stories, and especially their bodies.[8]

Later, Rebolledo is joined by the literary criticism of Catrióna Rueda Esquibel, Chicana queer author, who in 2009 published *With Her Machete in Her Hand: Reading Chicana Lesbians*, the first monograph dedicated solely to analyzing writings by this group of writers. In the following decade, however, J. Frank Galarte challenged the "sitio y lengua" of some Latina feminist spaces, such as MALCS, as not always welcoming him as a trans* masculine Chican@ feminist. In calling out the organization's trans*phobia, Galarte offered his own embodied theory of "*el sabor del amor y del dolor*" (the taste/flavor of love and pain), which "acknowledges emotions as the decolonizing *movida* that can push us to consider new *sitios y lenguas*" where transphobia and the violence associated with it are acknowledged and eradicated. Galarte utilized Anzaldúa's declaration in *Borderlands / La Frontera* that everyone responds in similar manners to "pain and pleasure" and proposed that therefore it is time to experience some discomfort as the conversations push the boundaries of "un sitio y una lengua."

At the turn of the last century, there were also several other queer scholars who published important anthologies addressing the flourishing of Chicanx and Latinx queer scholarship. These works included several groundbreaking monographs and anthologies such as José Esteban Muñoz's *Disidentifications* (1999) and *Cruising Utopia* (2009); Marysol Asencio's *Sex and Sexuality Among New York's Puerto Rican Youth* (2002); Michael Hames-García and Ernesto Javier Martínez's *Gay Latino Studies* (2011); Carlos Ulises Decena's *Tacit Subjects* (2011); Lawrence La Fountain-Stokes's *Queer Ricans* (2009); and Juana María Rodríguez's *Queer Latinidad* (2003), among others.

Chicanx and Latinx literary and cultural productions continue to evolve as feminists, queers, and trans people, as well as heteronormative authors and artists, produce new literary and cultural endeavors. They, and we, continue to produce work for and with our communities. Our stories may still not be at the center of the U.S. imaginary, but thanks to the foundational work of the authors and cultural producers outlined in this chapter, our communities have better access to our stories. As a college student, you and your Chicanx and Latinx peers are now responsible for researching and writing about the works in which you see yourselves represented.

How We Write: "Research Is Me-Search"

While attending graduate school at the University of California, San Diego, some of us learned the phrase "research is me-search," which encouraged us to look for ourselves and/or our communities in the research we conducted. Your Chicanx or Latinx literature or culture topic will be most rewarding if you choose a theme that genuinely interests you, and one with which you identify. For example, if you (or members of your family) identify as an immigrant and/or queer from a particular place in the Americas, you may want to explore such aspects of your identity. Suppose you are an aspiring queer playwright from Ecuador. A broad topic such as theater or performance by queer authors from Ecuador would be a good starting topic. Yet, be-

FIGURE 3 Portrait of the jotx as Sor Juana Inés de la Cruz.

cause, like most initial "me-search" topics, this one is too broad to cover in a semester project, you would need to narrow it down. One of the best ways to do so is to visit your professors in office hours to have them help you with an initial brainstorming session. Beforehand, you might answer some of these questions:

What do you want to know about queer theater or poetry from Ecuador? Who are the authors you would like to research? What about their lives or their work do you want to focus on? With what poems, plays, or characters in their work do you identify or empathize and why?

When we narrow our topic, follow our curiosity, and begin to excavate the details of the works that matter to us, we are on our way to producing the types of research and writing that transform our lives and, in turn, our communities. In order to honor our work and our communities, we must learn the tools of our craft: critical steps to producing critical texts with the potential to give back to our communities. Asking engaging questions allows us produce decolonizing essays that contribute to self and community empowerment. Quoting Gloria Anzaldúa, "May we [write] work that matters. Vale la pena, it's worth the pain" ("Let Us Be" 313).[9] Below are steps and recommendations to aid you in becoming a critical and effective Chicana/o/e/x or Latina/o/e/x scholar and writer.

Research: Basic Steps

1. Choose a topic in which you see yourself, your family, or your community.
2. Research the writer(s)/artist(s), their time, and their work.
3. Select research sources.
4. Create a list of important terms, concepts, and characters.
5. Develop and polish your research question(s) to create a clear and concise thesis statement.

Step One: Choose a Topic in Which You See Yourself, Your Family, or Your Community

As a student in a Chicanx or Latinx literature or culture class, we hope that your first approach to a written or visual text is one of pleasure, connection, and/or excitement. This energy will later provide you with the vigor to research, write, and rewrite—to transform your project into a well-crafted work of critical analysis. The first time your professor introduces you to a film, a novel, a play, or a work of visual art, allow yourself to simply enjoy it and learn about it without much pressure or concern. Be sure to jot down brief notes, key words, or phrases about the work that speak to you. After you have allowed yourself to enjoy the material, return to it a second time and take more detailed notes, focusing on the aspects of the work that move you. This exercise may result in several pages of notes, and at this point you can narrow down your topic. Read through your notes for common themes and be sure to either highlight those ideas or rewrite your notes, focusing on either the most common themes or the ones most important to you. These will be the topics where you later focus your analysis.

Step Two: Research the Writer(s)/Artist(s), Their Time, and Their Work

In order to understand a work, often it is recommended that we understand the artist or author, but not all literary approaches require this step. The political climate of our (or any given) time, the families in which we are raised, and our sex, race, and gender all may have some influence on the work we produce. Detailing the sociopolitical and historical backgrounds to a cultural production allows you to focus the discussion within the original time frame in which it was produced in order to avoid a "presentist" approach. Sometimes students want to write from their "present" or current sociopolitical situation, yet this may not be appropriate for the text(s) they are evaluating. While we all bring our values to our research, in order to hear the messages the author was trying to convey, we must identify and analyze historical or descriptive writings about the producers of these cultural works. Answer questions such as: Who are these writers/authors/artists and what was their motivation for their creations? What did their society look like when they produced their work? What issues were they responding to? With what other work(s) are they engaging? You may not be able to find all these answers, but the more you read about the authors and their work, the stronger your essay will be. If you are having a difficult time finding such contextualizing materials, a librarian and your professor are available to guide your search. In addition, be sure to utilize the online sources you find in the back (appendices) of this text.

Step Three: Select Research Sources

In the age of technology, most students begin their preliminary research online with a simple Wikipedia or general Google search.[10] At times, these sources have useful bibliographies that are helpful for identifying sources, but Wikipedia is not a refereed source. That is to say, the essays found there are not reviewed by experts in the field, and should not be the sources you use in your research. In our fields of study, the requirement is for students to identify and utilize "peer-reviewed" or "refereed" works (such as articles, books, or chapters), which have undergone a rigorous assessment process by experts in the author's academic field. These anonymous reviewers determine whether the essay contains accurate information and whether it is publishable as written or merits revisions before publication. As you can infer, because the writing process works best when it is collaborative, even famous writers and scholars must have their essays reviewed by other experts. Most assignments will require you to engage with a number of refereed publications to sustain and validate your argument. When in doubt, again, ask a librarian or your professor if a source is peer-reviewed. Excellent examples of scholarly and peer-reviewed journals in Chicanx and Latinx studies are *Chicana/Latina Studies: The Journal of Mujeres Activas en Letras y*

Cambio Social, Aztlán: A Journal of Chicano Studies, and *Latino Studies.* Because one objective is for Latinx and Chicanx students to have access to such scholarly work, the journal *Chicana/Latina Studies* has made their publications (except for the last four volumes published at any given time) available, free of charge, on the website This Bridge Called Cyberspace.[11]

Step Four: Create a List of Important Terms, Concepts, and Characters

As you read through your sources, begin to take notes and create lists of important terms, concepts, or ideas, and of the characters that move the story. At the same time, write down quotations that speak to you and that you may want to utilize in your essay. As you note the quotations, be sure to mark them as such with quotation marks. When you turn in a paper, all quotations must be clearly marked, or, for longer block quotations, indented (see appendix C for MLA details). Marking all quotations will help you reduce the risk of accidental plagiarism. In research essays, all quotations need to be cited, in the text, in the Modern Language Association (MLA) style, which requires the author's or authors' last name(s) followed by the page number. Leave out the page number if no pagination is available. This information must be in parentheses following the quotation. Examples of how to do this are found in appendix C of this volume.

Because you will have several sources from which you are gathering your research, it is critical to write down where these terms, concepts, characters, and quotations are located. Include titles of works, authors, and page numbers so that the information is easily available to you when you begin writing. Whether this information is on notecards, in a notebook, or on your computer is up to you, but be sure to keep all your notes together in one place. It will make it easy to later cite your work in your paper. As you are collecting and reading these materials, it is never too early to add them to your bibliography or "Works Cited" page. Once your paper is drafted, you can edit this list of sources and narrow them down to only the ones you use.

Step Five: Develop and Polish Your Research Question(s) to Create a Clear and Concise Thesis Statement

Once you have gathered your research notes, you are ready to draft your research question(s). Begin by asking questions such as: What about these materials matters most to me and why? What aspects of my findings do I want to explore or engage with? How can these ideas/materials challenge social norms, heteronormativity, racism, transphobia, or xenophobia? Julieta Paredes Carvajal, an Aymara feminist, activist, poet, writer, graffiti artist, and musician from Bolivia, created the term "despatriarcalización/depatriarchalization," which means the decentering, contesting, and dismantling of the patriarchal structures that support and sustain transnational economic systems of oppression (Paredes Carvajal 100). How does your work depatriarchalize? Make a list of other questions you would like to answer that engage with the materials. Do not ask questions that are too broad for one essay or that have yes or no answers. There should be some questions that are perfect for a research paper. Often it helps to organize, focus, and/or narrow your questions by brainstorming and talking with a friend or colleague. Finally, be sure to match your research questions with sources that will help you answer them, and stay focused throughout your writing process.

The Writing Process at a Glance

1. First things first.
2. Draft your thesis.
3. Create an outline.
4. Draft your essay.

5. Revise your essay.
6. Give back to the community.

Writing an essay for a course on Chicanx/Latinx literature and culture means that sometimes you will incorporate several other fields of study such as history, sociology, anthropology, or communication studies into your essay. This form of writing is called interdisciplinary, and often your professors for these courses have undergone rigorous training to become experts in combining and utilizing various disciplines in their own writing. At the same time, in these courses, you will learn to focus exclusively on a primary source, such as a novel, a short story, a painting, a film, a play, or a poem, in order to practice the "close reading" of such texts.[12] By honing your attention to form or structure, phrases or word choices, bilingualism, or cultural identifiers, you are able to explore and excavate possible meanings the authors sought to convey. As you approach a text, take careful notes on what you find striking or interesting; the information you gather will be critical when you begin to interpret the work.

Another strategy before beginning your draft is to develop an annotated bibliography of the sources you found while conducting research. This method consists of writing five or six detailed sentences that summarize the contents of each article, book, and any other source you identified as useful. Because an annotated bibliography is exactly what the name implies, the information you gathered during your research regarding the author, publisher, and other bibliographic details will help you draft this list of sources. For our purposes in this chapter, examples and details are in MLA style to help you organize your sources.[13] Keep in mind that annotated bibliographies can stand alone as a separate assignment when a professor staggers the steps to a research paper or essay. These detailed summaries not only help you organize and develop your ideas, they also make it easier to choose your texts accordingly as you set out upon drafting your essay and as you revise your work.

Step One: First Things First

College writing, in summary, is about learning how to build a sound, believable, and convincing argument, which should be written with clarity while avoiding the use of colloquial language. As you transition from high school to higher education, you will notice that your writing is about joining an ongoing conversation or discussion. Generations before you began conversations about justice, culture, community, beauty, and more. It is important to remember that you are never "late" to these exchanges, and as you take various classes and practice writing regularly, you will gain more confidence as you participate in academic discourse. Remember, everyone started somewhere, and your professors and college resource offices/centers will help you enter these academic conversations. If, as recommended above, you choose a topic that inspires you and that is important to you and/or your community, it will help you as you work through the following steps. The steps you find below will aid you in demonstrating to others why your topic is important to you, your community, and your readers. Be explicit about your motivations and let your readers know why you think your essay is worth reading. Assert your ideas and be proud of your contributions; few students are going to have your unique perspective given your intersectionality. By virtue of who you are, you will be producing "writing that matters" with the support of your professors, peers, and community. Writing can be a lonely endeavor, but once you connect with a writing community in or outside your classrooms, the process becomes easier and more enjoyable.

Step Two: Draft Your Thesis

Drafting your thesis, or argument, is often the most difficult task of the writing process, because you must go beyond description and detailed observations. Your thesis must be a statement (in one or two succinct, clear sentences) with which others could agree or disagree. Using persuasive reasoning, supported by convincing evidence, your thesis should bring together a statement that draws your reader into your paper. It must be supported by sound ideas or assumptions that your audience will follow in agreement or disagreement. It is sometimes referred to as "conclusions plus reasons plus assumptions." Finally, do not assume that every reader will understand your key terms. If you utilize field-specific terms in your thesis, you will need to define them when you introduce your thesis. For example, in our fields of study, often we define the terms we use to name our ethnicity or gender identities (see chapter 1, "We Name Ourselves").

Thesis Statement Examples:

- During the grape strike of 1965–1970, the symbol of the Virgin of Guadalupe served to unite workers in their struggle for justice.

- Written in the late twentieth century, Rosaura Sánchez and Beatrice Pita's *Lunar Braceros* functions as a critique of environmental exploitation.

Step Three: Create an Outline

Your argument or thesis will define the way you structure your essay, and in college you will no longer use the five-paragraph method you learned in secondary school. Instead, your essays will be much longer, more detailed, and therefore more sophisticated. Because in college-length essays it is challenging to create a cohesive argument, working from an outline is critical. When you do not take the time to craft an outline, you risk creating a paper that wanders from idea to idea, theme to theme, instead of presenting a convincing argument. Your thesis, which must consist of "conclusions plus reasons plus assumptions," will serve as a guide in crafting an outline. It will give you a road map of what to argue and in what order. Depending on the length of your essay, your outline should consist of several main ideas or themes (three is a common number), and each theme must be supported by evidence from your research. Here is a simple essay outline:

I. Introduction.
    A. Interesting opening sentence that grabs the reader's attention.
    B. Context or background information.
    C. Thesis statement.

II. Theme 1.
    A. First main idea.
        a. First piece of supporting evidence and details.
        b. Second piece of supporting evidence and details.
    B. Second main idea.
        a. First piece of supporting evidence and details.
        b. Second piece of supporting evidence and details.

III. Themes 2 and beyond (repeat these "theme" steps as necessary).

IV. Conclusion.
    A. Give a synopsis of your argument.
    B. Remind readers of the importance of your themes (especially for your communities).
    C. Close with a strong, assertive sentence.

Step Four: Draft Your Essay

Once you have a working thesis and outline, it is time to begin drafting. Keep in mind, as you write, that your work must be descriptive and analytical. As you write, stay focused on your thesis and how each theme ties into it. Be sure that all claims are supported with evidence. If you find yourself using phrases like "I think," it may be because you do not have enough evidence to support that claim. Slow down and make sure you want to include that theme or argument in the paper. You may need to adjust your outline and/or your thesis. Remember that writing is "recursive"— that is, one step feeds into another or relates to another. As you write, make sure to make full use of your outline. At times, students key their draft directly into their outline. Other students prefer to keep a copy of their outline off to the side, jotting down new ideas as they arise. Using subtitles or subheadings can also be helpful while drafting your essay; they also guide the reader in a clear manner.

It is while you are drafting your paper that you also begin making use of the quotations you found during your research. These help to provide the support and evidence for the claims you are making. You will need to decide what material will be most effective when quoted directly, and what evidence will be best utilized if paraphrased, using your own words. Do not, however, use the quotations you selected to complete your own sentences, and do not leave the quotations to do your job or "speak" for you. Instead, set up a quotation, use it, and proceed to explain it, connecting it to your theme. Additionally, remember that literary and artistic works require interpretation; apply your close-reading skills (see endnote 12 for details of this activity) when appropriate. Your essay should be sophisticated, but not overly complex. Because we want to encourage you to make your writing accessible to our communities, perhaps you can think about how to ensure that someone in your family who has not gone to college can understand your ideas even if they do not understand everything in your essay.

Considering possible counterarguments is also an important part of drafting your paper. For every claim that you make, think of the disagreements that readers might have with them. Then engage with them and use your evidence to find your way to a suitable explanation or defense. Do not attempt to crush every disagreement with your argument and examples along the way; instead, embrace complex and interesting ideas. Become a clever "conversationalist" with your writing by being prepared and supporting all your claims with ample and interesting examples and evidence.

Step Five: Revise Your Essay

Once you have drafted your paper, be sure to proofread your work, making use of the Chicanx and Latinx Power Writing Rules found at the end of chapter 5. Check to make sure you have strong topic sentences for each of your paragraphs. Because "writing is rewriting" and the best of these practices is never done alone, once you have proofed your essay, share it. Find a family member, community member, or peer who can listen to you as you read it out loud. This step will help you keep your style of writing clear, concise, and accessible. With clarity and concision, your writing can achieve a complex and elegant style. Be sure to take your listener's or reader's feedback kindly and openly as you prepare to revise your essay. Do not be defensive or take offense if someone tells you that they cannot understand what you wrote. Go back and rewrite long sentences. If a paragraph is more than a third of a page in length, it is probably too long; it may contain more than one specific point or main idea. Relatedly, a paragraph that is less than three sentences may not offer enough evidence to support your theme. Double-space and print out your draft to take a quick glance at the size of your paragraphs. You can also write notes to yourself on the margins or in between the lines to make your revisions easier.

Most colleges or universities have staff that dedicate their work to the art of writing. Use these resources. Once you have read over your paper using the Power Writing Rules, shared it with a friend or family member, and considered their input, make time to visit your campus's writing center. They exist and were designed with you in mind. And remember, always: when in doubt about whether or not to cite someone else's ideas, ask your professor or the writing center's tutors. Plagiarism will result in serious academic trouble, and you can avoid it by proofing your citations and consulting your instructors.

Step Six: Give Back to the Community

After completing several drafts and sharing your essay, you will arrive at a final version of your work, which you will turn in to your professor. In turning it in, you become part of a larger conversation about our communities and our culture. In addition, however, consider sharing your work with a wider audience—using the power of your words and work to give back to our communities. Consider sharing your essay with your family or community members, thus bringing them into the conversation. Sometimes professors can invite you to participate in local or national conferences where you can engage other scholars and students with your research. Or perhaps you can volunteer to work with middle-school or high-school students who do not have access to Chicanx and Latinx literature and culture materials and share what you have learned with them. If you have peers who are visual learners, maybe they can help you transform your written research into a zine or a website.

DISCUSSION QUESTIONS

1. Why is it important to understand who belongs to the Chicanx and Latinx literary and cultural canon?
2. What were some examples of excavations or recoveries of our literary and cultural works? Why do they matter?
3. How was the work of Chicana/Latina feminists, queer ones in particular, foundational for these fields of study?
4. How did the first literary anthologies promote the work of Chicanx and Latinx authors, poets, and artists?

5. What are some of the themes that Puerto Rican and Chicanx literature have in common?

6. What does it mean to "depatriarchalize"?

7. What is a peer-reviewed or refereed publication, and why are they important?

8. Why is it important to write clearly and accessibly?

9. For Chicanx and Latinx students of literature and culture, why is close reading important?

10. Why do we say that "writing is rewriting," and why should you share your essay drafts?

11. After you complete the first draft of a research paper, what should you *always* do?

12. In what ways can Chicanx and Latinx students of literature and culture share their work with their communities?

WORKS CITED (MLA STYLE)

Aldama, Frederick Luis. *The Routledge Concise History of Latino/a Literature*. Routledge, 2013.

Allende, Isabel. *La casa de los espíritus*. Plaza & Janés, 1982.

Allende, Isabel. *The House of the Spirits*. Translated by Magda Bogin, Knopf, 1985.

Almaguer, Tomás. "Chicano Men: A Cartography of Homosexual Identity and Behavior." *Journal of Feminist Cultural Studies*, vol. 3, no. 2, Summer 1991, pp. 75–100.

Alvarez, Julia. *In the Time of the Butterflies*. Algonquin Books of Chapel Hill, 1994.

Anzaldúa, Gloria E. *Borderlands / La Frontera: The New Mestiza*. Aunt Lute Books, 1987.

Anzaldúa, Gloria E. "Let Us Be the Healing of the Wound." *The Gloria Anzaldúa Reader*, edited by AnaLouise Keating, Duke UP, 2009, pp. 303–17.

Anzaldúa, Gloria E., editor. *Making Face, Making Soul / Haciendo Caras: Creative and Critical Perspectives by Women of Color*. Aunt Lute Books, 1990.

Anzaldúa, Gloria E., and AnaLouise Keating. *This Bridge We Call Home: Radical Visions for Transformation*. Routledge, 2002.

Arrizón, Alicia. *Latina Performance: Traversing the Stage*. Indiana UP, 1999.

Asencio, Marysol. *Sex and Sexuality Among New York's Puerto Rican Youth*. Lynne Rienner Publishers, 2002.

Castañeda, Antonia, and Clara Lomas, editors. *Writing/Righting History: Twenty-Five Years of Recovering the US Hispanic Literary Heritage*. Arte Público Press, 2019.

Castillo, Ana. "Interview with Ana Castillo." Interview by Marta A. Navarro. *Chicana Lesbians: The Girls Our Mothers Warned Us About*, edited by Carla Trujillo, Third Woman Press, 1991, pp. 113–32.

Castillo, Ana. *The Invitation*. Self-published, 1986.

Castillo, Ana. *The Mixquiahuala Letters*. Bilingual Press, 1986.

Castro, Nívea. "Tatiana de la tierra: The ¿Cuándo Supiste? Interview, 9 June 2012." *Sinister Wisdom*, no. 97, Summer 2015.

Cisneros, Sandra. *The House on Mango Street*. Arte Público Press, 1983.

Cisneros, Sandra. *My Wicked Wicked Ways*. Third Woman Press, 1987.

Cotto-Thorner, Guillermo. *Manhattan Tropics / Trópico en Manhattan*. Edited by J. Bret Maney and Cristina Pérez Jiménez, translated by J. Bret Maney, Arte Público Press, 2019.

Decena, Carlos Ulises. *Tacit Subjects: Belonging and Same-Sex Desire Among Dominican Immigrant Men*. Duke UP, 2011.

de la Selva, Salomón. *Tropical Town and Other Poems*. Arte Público Press, 1999.

de la tierra, tatiana. *For the Hard Ones: A Lesbian Phenomenology / Para las duras: Una fenomenología lesbiana*. Calaca Press, 2002.

Esquibel, Catrióna Rueda. *With Her Machete in Her Hand: Reading Chicana Lesbians*. U of Texas P, 2006.

Galarte, J. Frank. "Notes from a Trans* Chicana/o Survivor." *Mujeres Talk Blog*, 24 October 2011, http://mujerestalk.org/tag/trans/.

García, Cristina. *Dreaming in Cuban*. Ballantine Books, 1993.

Gaspar de Alba, Alicia. "Thirty Years of Chicana/Latina Lesbian Literary Production." *The Routledge Companion to Latino/a Literature*, edited by Suzanne Bost and Frances R. Aparicio, Routledge, 2015, pp. 462–75.

Goodwin, Matthew David, editor. *Latinx Rising: An Anthology of Science Fiction and Fantasy*. Mad Creek Books, 2020.

Gutiérrez, Ramón A. "Community, Patriarchy and Individualism: The Politics of Chicano History and the Dream of Equality." *American Quarterly*, vol. 45, no. 1, March 1993, pp. 44–72.

Hames-García, Michael, and Ernesto Javier Martínez. "Introduction: Re-membering Gay Latino Studies." *Gay Latino Studies: A Critical Reader*, edited by Michael Hames-García and Ernesto Javier Martínez, Duke UP, 2011, pp. 1–18.

Heidenreich, L. "Introduction." *Nepantla²: Transgender Mestiz@ Histories in Times of Global Shift*, U of Nebraska P, 2021.

Hernández Linares, Leticia, Rubén Martínez, and Héctor Tobar, editors. *The Wandering Song: Central American Writings in the United States*. Tia Chucha Press, 2017.

Horno-Delgado, Asunción, Eliana Ortega, Nina M. Scott, and Nancy Saporta-Sternbach, editors. *Breaking Boundaries: Latina Writing and Critical Readings*. U of Massachusetts P, 1989.

Leal, Luis. "A Historical Perspective." *A Luis Leal Reader*, edited by Ilan Stavans, Northwestern UP, 2007, pp. 14–27.

Leal, Luis. "The Problem of Identifying Chicano Literature." *A Luis Leal Reader*, edited by Ilan Stavans, Northwestern UP, 2007, pp. 28–32.

Merla-Watson, Cathryn Josefina, and B. V. Olguín, editors. *Altermundos: Latin@ Speculative Literature, Film and Popular Culture*. U of Washington P, 2017.

Moraga, Cherríe. *Giving Up the Ghost*. West End Press, 1991.

Moraga, Cherríe, and Gloria Anzaldúa, editors. *This Bridge Called My Back: Writings By Radical Women of Color*. Persephone Press, 1981.

Moraga, Cherríe, and Ana Castillo, editors. *Esta puente, mi espalda: Voces de mujeres tercermundistas en los Estados Unidos*. ISM Press, 1988.

Muñoz, José Esteban. *Cruising Utopia: The Then and There of Queer Futurity*. New York UP, 2009.

Muñoz, José Esteban. *Disidentifications: Queers of Color and the Performance of Politics*. U of Minnesota P, 1999.

Muñoz, Miguel Elías. *Crazy Love*. Arte Público Press, 1989.

Paredes Carvajal, Julieta. "Despatriarcalización: Una respuesta categórica del feminismo comunitario (descolonizando la vida)." *Bolivian Studies Journal / Revista de Estudios Bolivianos*, vol. 21, no. 100, March 2016, pp. 100–115.

Pérez, Emma. "Sexuality and Discourse: Notes from a Chicana Survivor." *Chicana Lesbians: The Girls Our Mothers Warned Us About*, edited by Carla Trujillo, Third Woman Press, 1991, pp. 159–84.

Ramos, Juanita, editor. *Compañeras: Latina Lesbians*. Routledge, 1994.

Rebolledo, Tey Diana. *Women Singing in the Snow: A Cultural Analysis of Chicana Literature*. U of Arizona P, 1996.

Rebolledo, Tey Diana, and Eliana S. Rivero, editors. *Infinite Divisions: An Anthology of Chicana Literature*. U of Arizona P, 1993.

Reyes, Rodrigo, Francisco X. Alarcón, and Juan Pablo Gutiérrez. *Ya Vas Carnal*. Humanizarte Publications, 1985.

Rodríguez, Juana María. *Queer Latinidad: Identity Practices, Discursive Spaces*. New York UP, 2003.

Ruiz de Burton, María Amparo. *The Squatter and the Don*. Edited and introduced by Rosaura Sánchez and Beatrice Pita, Arte Público Press, 1997.

Ruiz de Burton, María Amparo. *Who Would Have Thought It?* Edited and introduced by Rosaura Sánchez and Beatrice Pita, Arte Público Press, 1995.

Sánchez, Rosaura, and Rosa Martínez Cruz, editors. *Essays on La Mujer*. Chicano Studies Center Publications, 1977.

Sánchez, Rosaura, and Beatrice Pita. *Keep Me Posted: Logins from Tomorrow*. Floricanto Press, 2020.

Sánchez, Rosaura, and Beatrice Pita. *Lunar Braceros 2125–2148*. Calaca Press, 2009.

Soto, Sandra. *Reading Chican@ Like a Queer: The Demastery of Desire*. U of Texas P, 2010.

Trujillo, Carla, editor. *Chicana Lesbians: The Girls Our Mothers Warned Us About.* Third Woman Press, 1991.

Umpierre, Luz María. *The Margarita Poems.* Third Woman Press, 1987.

Viramontes, Helena María. *The Moths and Other Stories.* Arte Público Press, 1995.

FURTHER READING

Alarcón, Norma. "Chicana's Feminist Literature: A Re-Vision through Malintzin / or Malintzin: Putting Flesh Back on the Object." In *This Bridge Called My Back: Writings by Radical Women of Color,* edited by Cherríe Moraga and Gloria Anzaldúa, 2nd ed., 182–90. New York: Kitchen Table Press, 1983.

Aldama, Frederick Luis. *The Routledge Concise History of Latino/a Literature.* New York: Routledge, 2013.

Anzaldúa, Gloria E. *Borderlands / La Frontera: The New Mestiza.* San Francisco: Aunt Lute Books, 1987.

Arrizón, Alicia. *Latina Performance: Traversing the Stage.* Bloomington: Indiana University Press, 1999.

Arrizón, Alicia, and Lillian Manzor, eds. *Latinas on Stage: Practice and Theory.* Berkeley: Third Woman Press, 2000.

Esquibel, Catrióna Rueda. *With Her Machete in Her Hand: Reading Chicana Lesbians.* Austin: University of Texas Press, 2006.

Gaspar de Alba, Alicia. "Thirty Years of Chicana/Latina Lesbian Production." In *Routledge Companion to Latino/a Literature,* edited by Suzanne Bost and Frances R. Aparicio, 462–75. London: Routledge, 2015.

Hames-García, Michael Roy, and Ernesto Javier Martínez, eds. *Gay Latino Studies: A Critical Reader.* Durham: Duke University Press, 2011.

La Fountain-Stokes, Lawrence. "Queering Latina/o Literature." In *The Cambridge Companion to Latina/o American Literature,* edited by John Morán González, 178–94. New York: Cambridge University Press, 2016.

La Fountain-Stokes, Lawrence. *Queer Ricans: Cultures and Sexualities in the Diaspora.* Minneapolis: University of Minnesota Press, 2009.

Moraga, Cherríe. *Giving Up the Ghost.* Albuquerque: West End Press, 1991.

Moraga, Cherríe, and Gloria E. Anzaldúa, eds. *This Bridge Called My Back: Writings by Radical Women of Color.* New York: Kitchen Table Press, 1981.

Ramos, Juanita, ed. *Compañeras: Latina Lesbians.* New York: Routledge, 1987.

Sánchez, Rosaura, and Rosa Martínez Cruz, eds. *Essays on La Mujer.* Los Angeles: Chicano Studies Center Publications, University of California, Los Angeles, 1977.

Soto, Sandra K. *Reading Chican@ Like a Queer: The Demastery of Desire.* Austin: University of Texas Press, 2010.

Torres, Lourdes, and Pertusa Inmaculada, eds. *Tortilleras: Hispanic and U.S. Latina Lesbian Expression.* Philadelphia: Temple University Press, 2003.

Trujillo, Carla, ed. *Chicana Lesbians: The Girls Our Mothers Warned Us About.* Berkeley: Third Woman Press, 1991.

CHAPTER 4

Interviewing Like the Justice Scholar That I Am

Constructing Interviews, Oral Histories, and Pláticas

> Speaking history connects generations. Speaking history simultaneously reflects both the multinodal worlds of the narrator and the interviewer. The consequences of oral history are lessons which the students and the instructor carry with them long after the tape recorders click off.
>
> —VICKI RUIZ, "SITUATING STORIES"

nterviews have played a central role in Chicanx/Latinx studies from the founding of our fields. They can serve to bring resources from the university to the community and, at the same time, create a means for the community to shape and influence the university. As noted in the epigraph that opens this chapter, these tools are also critical because they connect us to our elders and antepasadas/os with words that are active: our words and the words of others—sometimes called narrators, sometimes testimoniantes, interviewees, or subjects—come together in a conversation. If we craft our questions carefully and in dialogue with interviewees, the conversation becomes dynamic, with both speaker and interviewer taking the words, energy, and experience with them "long after the [recording devices] are clicked off."

One of the founders of Chicanx studies, Raquel Rubio-Goldsmith, noted that interviews are critical to our fields for another reason: in researching the histories of Chicanx and Latinx communities, often written sources are not enough. Rubio-

Goldsmith found that archival sources often left our histories incomplete, noting:

> My search had begun in libraries and archives—repositories of traditional history. The available sources were to be found in census reports, church records, directories, and other such statistical information. These, however, as important as they are cannot provide one of the essential dimensions of history, the full narrative of the human experience that defies quantification and classification.[1]

Whether they are oral history, plática, or testimonio, interviews aid us in learning a fuller "narrative of the human experience." While no history or interview can ever tell the whole story, they can help us reach a more complete understanding of the past and the present.

In this chapter, we address interviews and their multiple uses, the process for conducting them, and the ways in which Chicanx and Latinx scholars and communities have utilized these tools in scholarly production and for community empowerment. We address recorded interviews in detail, making note of extra steps you will need to take if crafting a plática. After we map and explain the art of the interview, we then address two variations on the interview: the plática and the testimonio. Whether you are conducting an oral history, facilitating a plática, or taking or speaking a testimonio, many of the tools you need will be similar. Thus, the key steps you must follow for any of these methods are addressed in the "Interviews" section below. At the heart of all these forms of knowledge production is listening.

Interviews

As noted by historian Lorena Márquez, oral history, as a method, has its roots in the traditional disciplines of anthropology, history, and sociology. During the era of the liberation movements (1950s–70s), interviews and oral histories became a critical tool for scholars who sought to fill in the gaps found in written and print sources.[2] African American and Chicanx scholars were at the forefront of this movement. In fact, historian Vicki L. Ruiz made extensive use of oral histories in *Cannery Women, Cannery Lives*, the first monograph of Chicana history published by a university press.[3] It is by looking both to the work of the founders of our field, such as Ruiz, Rubio-Goldsmith, and the Latina Feminist Group, and to that of later generations, such as Márquez, that we are able to produce a blueprint for writing ethical, useful, and productive interviews.

As with research working from print sources, interviews require preliminary work. Building on the work of Chicana scholars, as well as a folklorist by the name of Edward Ives, we can identify specific and critical steps for successful interviews. Respect and self-reflection are critical to this type of work.

Critical Preliminary Steps
1. Begin keeping a log.
2. Study and get to know the broader community and historical context.
3. Identify and reflect on your social location.
4. Identify and recognize your assumptions about the topic, community, and/or event.
5. Craft preliminary questions.
6. Complete human subject permission forms.

Begin Keeping a Log

Keeping a notebook throughout your research is critical for several reasons: it will allow you to see how your research process changes and develops your understanding of a topic and/or your community; it will remind you of the context of the interviews when you return to transcribe your recordings, and later to write your paper; and it will provide context for scholars who utilize the interview transcripts in the future. For some scholars, the easiest way to keep a record or log is to use a composition notebook as they move through the project. Many contemporary scholars prefer to use electronic notebooks or various types of software. The critical rule is to begin logging your activities and thoughts as soon as you have solidified your topic.

Study and Get to Know the Broader Community and Historical Context

We conduct interviews to learn about a specific event or person. Yet people and events exist in a specific time and space. Context research aids you in crafting stronger interview questions and shows respect to the people with whom you will be working. Thus, before crafting questions and before speaking with subjects, you must research the broader history and context of your topic. If you are conducting interviews as part of a class, the professor may provide some of this material for you. At other times you will have to do much of the context research yourself.

As a specific example, the founding of the Women's Caucus of the Young Lords Party is a perfect topic for exploring the importance of context research. Before beginning your paperwork for permissions or drafting possible questions, you would learn everything you could about the Women's Caucus, the Young Lords Party (and the Young Lords Organization), and the history of the United States in relationship to Puerto Rico.[4] You would need to identify major watershed moments in the history of Puerto Rican resistance to U.S. imperialism and create a timeline to remind yourself of these important events. When shifting your gaze to the mainland in this history, you would note multiple critical moments such as the granting of limited U.S. citizenship to Puerto Ricans, and the great migration in which one-third of the population of the Island immigrated to the mainland. In the founding of the Young Lords Party (YLP) you would note a split from the original Young Lords Organization, and the strong influence of allies such as the Black Panthers; you would also note a shift in how the YLP addressed machismo within the organization and their own communities. From this larger context, initial interview questions might emerge, such as: Who inspired the women of the Women's Caucus? How did the leadership of Denise Oliver or Iris Morales influence how the women of the caucus saw/experienced their role in the organization? Which actions or projects did you find most rewarding?[5] Preliminary research allows you to craft informed questions that demonstrate your respect for your interviewees and their labor; it will also make your questions more useful to you and future generations, because you will not spend much time on questions that can be answered by print material.

Identify Your Own Social Location in Relation to the Topic, Community, or Event and Reflect on the Power Relationships Involved in Your Work

Our social locations are complex; this makes our relationship to our research and to our interviewees complex. While historians and sociologists often speak of insider/outsider relationships, most research relationships are much more complicated than such a dichotomy suggests.[6] For example: I, L Heidenreich, am ethnically mixed Euro-Chican@, and genderqueer, and a graduate of private and parochial schools, and the child of a custodial worker; I grew up below the poverty line but am now middle class. These vectors of myself exist simultaneously and affect my relationship with the people I interview. When I interview other Chicanxs, I have some things in common with them but also hold many different perspectives; similarly, when I interview other Euro-Americans, I have some things in common with them but also hold different experiences and perspectives. Patricia Zavella, a Chicana feminist anthropologist writing in the 1990s, explained it this way: "We should realize that we are almost always simultaneous insiders and outsiders."[7] As we prepare to do the work of interviewing, we need to engage in self-reflection and consider our relationships to the events we are writing about and the people with whom we will be speaking.

As scholars with access to higher education, we also must remind ourselves that we benefit from the work we are doing.[8] The time and emotional energy our subjects share benefit us, whether it be in tangible forms such as our grades or publications, or intangible forms like building within us a pride in our communities and a more robust understanding of the past. As noted by Vicki Ruiz, reciprocity is critical to any oral history project.[9] Reflecting on what we are receiving from this work will help form a base from which we can build a positive working relationship with our interviewees—even when the interviewees are our family members.

Identify and Recognize Your Own Assumptions

Even when we approach topics related to our home communities, we often do so with feelings and assumptions about the event, time, or person. Are you researching the first Latina to run for city council in your hometown? If so, you might approach interviews with pride and expect to hear very positive things about the person and their campaign. Reflecting on these feelings and expectations in your log/journal will anchor your work with a starting point and mark the emotional energy with which you approach the work. It will also aid you in identifying the bias you bring to the project. As noted in chapter 2, each one of us brings a biased perspective to our work; thus it is important to be aware of our attitudes and biases. As you complete your preliminary research, your assumptions about the event may be challenged. You will also want to log changes in your understanding of the event.

Craft Questions and Ask Permission

CRAFTING QUESTIONS

In conducting Chicanx and Latinx research, it is critical to include interviewees in as many of the steps of your research as possible. As noted by Natalia Deeb-Sossa, "Trust and mutual respect take time."[10] If we want interviewees/narrators to share their stories with us, we must be sure to include them in the decision-making parts of the research process. Using the context research you completed to construct working questions and then asking subjects for input will demonstrate to your interviewees that you take your work and their labor seriously, and it will allow both of you to actively shape the interview. If you are crafting a plática, this is also critical—each participant must have the opportunity to comment on your preliminary questions. Keep in mind that on many campuses you are required to submit interview questions as part of the approval process before you meet with any interviewees/narrators. Thus, you may need to have preliminary questions approved by your institutional review board (IRB) *before* meeting with your subjects.

As with most aspects of scholarly work, there are several steps to crafting questions, and there is more than one type of question. Here we build on the work of Edward Ives, a folklorist who in the 1970s argued, and demonstrated, that the histories of working people are critical to knowing the world around us. Ives used three types of questions: preliminary, directed, and open-ended.[11] In time, his practices became standard for most people in his field and influenced others, such as those of us in Chicanx and Latinx studies. Below is an overview of his method as shaped and influenced by the work of Chicana scholars such as Patricia Zavella, Raquel Rubio-Goldsmith, and Lorena Márquez.

- **Introductory questions**: Introductory questions allow the interviewee to get to know you and make the interview process more comfortable for both of you.[12] The questions may be about where the interviewee grew up or went to school, or how long they have lived in the town where they reside. Short questions such as these also allow you to share brief information about yourself. This discussion often takes place as you work with the interviewee in developing the questions for the formal interview.

- **Directed/closed-ended questions**: Like preliminary questions, directed questions also have short answers, but they are directly related to your project. Questions that ask who, what, where, and when are directed questions. "When did you become involved in the Women's Caucus?" "Did you participate in marches?" "Which neighborhood did you do most of your work in?" All of these questions have relatively short answers. At the same time, they create possibilities for the speaker to take control of the interview and expand on the questions or move the discussion in new directions.

- **Open-ended questions**: Most of the interview will consist of open-ended questions. As Ives explains, this is the heart of the interview. In drafting your questions, you will need to have several that allow the interviewee to speak expansively, questions such as: Why did you become involved in the Young Lords Party? What were some of the biggest challenges in community organizing? What are some of your strongest memories from that time? You will ask these questions after your introductory and directed questions. Finally, the last open-ended question you will need to ask is: Would you like to add anything else?

- Remember, these are working/draft questions. Prior to the formal interview you will meet with the speaker and discuss the questions. The draft questions allow you to complete IRB work and will provide you with critical material for your first meeting with the interviewee.

PERMISSIONS

There are two kinds of permissions that work together to keep our communities safe. The first is permissions from the institutional review boards (IRBs) at our colleges or universities; the second is from the interviewees. These two kinds of permission are related. IRBs require you to obtain permission from your interviewees, in part because doing so helps to protect the well-being of our communities.

Depending on your college or university, you may or may not have to complete an IRB form before speaking to interviewees. For example, we have a colleague who teaches a course in which students interview an elder member of their family about their life in the United States and the lessons they want to pass on to the next generation. For this class, because the questions are crafted with the aid of the professor and because each student is interviewing a family member, their review board has decided the students do not need forms completed for their work. For other classes, the campus IRB has required the professor to complete a form for the class. In that case each student does not need to complete a form. Because each campus has different policies regarding interviews and student projects, it is critical to check with your professor before you begin your project.

What are institutional review boards? IRBs are boards composed of established researchers who review any project that includes human beings. Their purpose is to keep research subjects safe and to protect the university from lawsuits. Historians trace the origins of IRBs to a troubled past, including late nineteenth-century vaccine experiments on children, Nazi medical experiments on humans during World War II, and the Tuskegee syphilis experiments on African Americans in the United States. The inhumane and violent treatment of Jews and other minorities by Nazi medical practitioners led to public, international trials of these medical practitioners and to a document called the Nuremberg Code. The code established three rules: all subjects involved in research must give their full and informed consent before participating in a study, any possible harm to participants must be minimized, and the study must somehow benefit the larger society.[13] These requirements shape all IRB regulations and processes.

In the United States another report influenced the procedures researchers now follow before they begin their research: the Belmont Report. Like the Nuremberg Code, the Belmont Report is the result of gross unethical behavior on the part of researchers. At the same time that Nazis experimented on minorities in Germany, U.S. physicians experimented on African American men in Tuskegee, Alabama. As noted by Joseph M. Verschaeve, "In this infamous scientific train wreck, U.S. government research scientists observed, but did not treat, syphilis among some of the 412 black men in the rural Alabama study. After the study was exposed and halted in 1972 a federal investigation concluded that at least 28 black men had died as a result of government doctors withholding treatment."[14]

Both the Nuremberg Code and the Belmont Report are the result of unethical behavior by medical practitioners. Authors of the reports addressed the practices of medical research but did not address the social sciences.[15] Nonetheless, today's IRBs base their criteria on these two reports. Thus, the three central principles of these documents affect the work that all academic scholars do and the standards to which IRBs hold all research: again, all subjects must give their informed consent, harm must be minimized, and the study must benefit the community and/ or the larger society. Without these three standards, it is too easy for researchers to do harm.

IRB Categories for Projects
Your IRB will have three categories for projects: exempt, expedited, or full board. Because it is difficult to know which set of paperwork to complete, this is yet another reason to make sure to work with your professor to complete this part of the project.

Many interview-based projects are considered "exempt." This does not mean that you do not have to complete any paperwork; instead, the paperwork you complete will be much shorter than that for other projects because there is less risk involved to the people with whom you will be working. You will still need to complete a consent form and other critical pieces of information, and someone at the IRB office will review your project before you meet with any interviewees. If your project might make the persons and/or communities involved vulnerable in any way, it might need a more thorough review, where members of the board, or even the full board, review the project and decide if you have sufficient safety measures to keep people safe. An example would be if you were interviewing people about activities that are considered illegal.

If you need to complete a form, do the following:

- **Work with your professor to complete the form.** IRB forms are several pages long. It is important to have an experienced mentor help you complete the form accurately.
- **State very clearly that the questions you are attaching are draft questions.** The form will ask you to list your interview questions. Be sure to include a statement that, once approved, you will meet with the interviewee to discuss the questions prior to the interview, and thus the questions may change.
- **State clearly whether or not the anonymity of the subjects will be protected.** IRB forms, because they were developed for medical research, ask how the subjects' anonymity will be protected. If yours is a history project, state clearly that the subject's identity will not be protected. State clearly that the interviewee is a significant actor in the history under study and the interview will not be anonymous. Instead, you will inform the subject of the archive or community center where the interview will be housed for use by future

scholars, and the interviewee will have an opportunity to
review the transcript before it is made public.

• If this is a sociology project where the names of the subjects
are not critical to the study, you must have a mechanism for
protecting the identity of your subjects. This task usually in-
volves the use of pseudonyms and a key that has the names
of your subjects with their pseudonyms. Once the study is
completed, you must destroy the key. You must also have a
secure place to store your interviews (a locked file cabinet
and/or a computer that only you have access to and that is
password protected).

• **Craft a release form** that is easily understandable and
meaningful to your interviewees. A release form explains
your project to your interviewee and asks their permission to use the interview in your project. You may also
include language granting permission to give the material
to an archive or community center. Even when a project is
deemed "exempt," you are responsible for crafting a release
form that your interviewee must sign before you begin
your interview. This is part of the process called "informed
consent," meaning that the interviewee understands
your project and how their words will be used. It is also
important that the interviewee understand all risks that
might be involved in speaking to you, including emotional
risks. Thus, it is critical that the form be written in clear
language. Look at the sample forms that your local IRB
has, but also imagine explaining your project to a family
member. With these two details in mind, draft your release
form. Make sure that your professor reviews the form
before you include it in your IRB application. If you are
interviewing people in a language other than English, make
sure you follow the appropriate steps for these documents
to be translated correctly. Ask your professor for details
regarding the topic of using other languages and whether

you will need to translate the entire interview or only the
quotations you use in your final project.

Conducting the Interview

PRELIMINARY MEETING

Before the preliminary meeting, contact the prospective interviewee by email or phone to see if they are willing to participate
in your project. Introduce yourself with one or two lines—for example, "I am a student in the Latinx studies program at XYZ college, who grew up in Quincey, Washington." Then in one or two
sentences explain why you are interested in your topic and why
the subject is important to the project. If an email, this should
be just a short paragraph. If a phone call, be sure to keep your
information brief as well. This is your very first contact with the
subject; the purpose of the phone call is to introduce the project
to the person and to ask permission to interview them. If they
agree, then you can move ahead to find a time when you can
meet for the preliminary meeting and/or interview.

At the preliminary meeting you get to know your subject and
they get to know you; you explain the project to them, even if
you have exchanged several emails prior to this time. It is in the
preliminary meeting that you ask permission to record the formal interview(s) and explain the transcription process. You also
review the release form with them carefully, explaining how the
interview will be shared and/or archived. If, after you discuss the
project with them, they no longer want to participate, be sure
to thank them for their time. Even when interviewing a family
member, it is still important to work with release forms and to
make sure that they clearly understand how their interview will
be used. Again, if they change their mind about participating,
thank them for their time and do not pursue the interview. Part
of informed consent is that interviewees choose to participate
without any pressure from the researcher.

Either during or before the preliminary meeting, be sure to review your draft questions with your interviewee. If the person has access to email, you may email them your questions ahead of time, asking them for edits and suggestions. When subjects do not have time to review questions prior to meeting, make time to review them during the first meeting. Be mindful that a subject might not have time for a separate preliminary interview. If so, it is important that when you plan the formal interview, you structure and mark off the first part of the interview for preliminary work.

MAIN INTERVIEW

Once you have clearly explained your project to your subject and they have agreed to work with you, set a time when the two of you can meet with as few interruptions as possible. Libraries with study rooms are an ideal site for interviews, but if you are interviewing an elder they may prefer their kitchen table or a more familiar space. In addition to a quiet area, you will need a recorder with good sound quality. Many departments and university media centers have digital recorders that you can borrow. Be sure to use a device that will allow you to transfer your files to your computer for transcription.

If the interview is in a public place, plan to arrive early so you have time to begin your journal entry by noting the environment where the interview will take place. What sounds do you hear? Is the environment warm? Spacious? Homey? Will you be at a desk or a kitchen table? Describe the environment in such a way that later researchers will be able to read your journal and imagine the space as they listen to your recording or read the transcript. If you interview in the home of the interviewee, leave space in the journal to enter this information at a later time. When I interviewed elders in my hometown I was able to record the interviews at my mother's kitchen table. This environment was ideal because it provided a homey space for the interviewees; at the same time it was a space with which I was familiar.

FIGURE 4 Table talking. Throughout the interview, direct your attention to your interviewee.

It also allowed interviewees to meet some of my family and see the space where I grew up. In short, it helped build trust in our working relationship.

Once the interviewee arrives, greet them and ask if they need anything and if they have any questions. Then start the recording by stating the date. Doing this will let them know that the recorder is now on. Normally, as an interview proceeds, both speaker and interviewer become more relaxed and the conversation will begin to flow. Remind yourself that your goal is to learn as much about the experience of your speaker as possible (and you are going to have to transcribe the interview)—try to keep your own words to a minimum. If you are crafting a plática, it is critical that you have each speaker introduce themselves. As they speak, jot down the name of each participant. One of the challenges of transcribing a plática is recognizing each speaker's voice during the course of the conversation.

Throughout the interview, direct your attention to your interviewee. Do not try to write down what each person says word for word (the recorder takes care of that task); instead, write down key points to remind yourself of the conversation. Note changes in the environment, especially those that transform the flow of the conversation. Does a librarian knock on the door to say the library is about to close? Does a grandchild wander into the room looking for a lap to sit on? Write these actions in your journal. These notes will serve as an important backup if sections of the recording are not clear; they may also help you to focus on key points made by the interviewee(s). Your notebook provides context for you and for anyone who accesses the work at a later date. Many archives will store the researcher's notebook with transcripts and/or recordings. Once the ideas and memories begin to flow, it is often best to let the speaker(s) drive the conversation. That is, if they begin to remember events you did not consider when crafting interview questions, it is best not to direct them back to the original question.

TRANSCRIBING

While at first glance it might seem tedious, transcription is a critical part of working with interviews. As you transcribe, you once again engage in active listening, and multiple senses come into play. If you work with transcription software that uses a pedal, you listen with your ears, type with your hands, and manage a device to move the recording forward and backward; your body works with the words as you move through the interview.

Be sure to read over your log before you begin transcribing. Reading will help you remember the context of the interview and contribute to a more accurate transcription. Before you begin transcribing, also be sure to type the date and interview information at the top of your page:

Subject interviewed by [your full name]
Location
Date

Rita E. Urquijo-Ruiz, interviewed by L Heidenreich
Pups and Cups Coffee Shop, Pullman, WA
13 Oct. 2021

Once you have done this, you are ready to begin typing. If you are going to manually transcribe the interview (if you have strong typing skills, this may be preferred), make sure to ask your professor to borrow a transcription kit, or foot pedal. These devices plug into your computer so that your hands are free to keep typing while you use your foot to move the recording forward and backward. Most pedals will allow you to adjust the play speed of the recording depending on the pressure you apply to the pedal. It may take a while to develop a rhythm, so be patient with yourself and your technology. As you proceed and find a play speed that works for you, you will find that you need to back up less. Allow yourself to enjoy this process. Transcribing often brings back rich memories of the interview. As you encounter pauses in the transcript, use brackets to note any events or micro-events that took place during the interview. This part is where your log will be helpful in remembering the context. For example, "[sibling entered the room and said hello]." While it is important to note pauses, you do not need to key in filler words such as "um."

Today, there are tools such as Otter, or the voice dictation tool on MS Word, that are useful for creating rough drafts. You simply record an interview with a mobile phone and then play the recording with your software running. The software produces a draft as the computer "listens" to the interview. You then save the document as your working/rough draft. If you use this method, be sure to return to the draft to fill in any critical information that is missing. Your software may not mark pauses, and you will need to key in details regarding events and micro-events. I have found that when I use this fabulous software for the initial drafting of a transcript, I need to return, read over the draft, add punctuation, and correct errors. Transcription software makes errors when an interview is in Spanglish, or Caló. For example, MS Word's dictation software transcribes "sabes que" as "salads gay." While this is a fabulous error, it does not convey the intended meaning of the speaker as "you know that."

Once you have a working draft of your transcript, there are a couple more steps to tend to. Whether you key the transcript in manually or use dictation software, always set aside a complete transcription and return to it a day or so later with fresh eyes for a second proofreading. In addition, there is always a chance that you or the software will not be able to understand the full conversation. If there are phrases or sections of the interview that are unclear, you will need to meet again with the interviewee to review the transcript and ask for clarification. Make sure the transcript is as polished as possible before meeting with the interviewee. If the transcript is clear and complete, then provide a copy to the interviewee for their records with an invitation for them to comment. Include a note thanking them for their time, labor, and willingness to share their story/history with you. Now you are ready to begin using your transcript as a primary source (see chapter 2 for working with primary sources).[16]

Pláticas

The space we create with pláticas requires that we, too, be open to sharing our own stories and be vulnerable as we are asking of contributors.

—FIERROS AND DELGADO BERNAL, 2016

When you hear the word *plática*, you may think of hanging out with friends, or sitting around the table with family at home, chatting/platicando about your day and good or difficult memories. The plática, as a tool and a research method, is rooted in this very personal kind of conversation. While crafting a plática will have much in common with crafting an interview, it also has some characteristics that make it unique as a tool of research and knowledge production. When you facilitate a plática you need to follow all the steps for conducting an interview, but there will be some differences. As noted in the discussion of interviews, pláticas sometimes have more than one interviewee/contributor; thus, extra care must be taken to note who is speaking as you take notes during the plática. Yet there are also structural differences to attend to when working with this powerful tool.

At the heart of the plática is sharing and openness. Building on the work of Ramón Calle and Lydia Mendoza, Dolores Delgado Bernal and Cindy O. Fierros mapped three parts to a plática: entrada, amistad, and despedida.[17]

- **Entrada**: Like the preliminary interview, this is a time of introduction. Qualitatively, it is different in that you want to take the time to get to know the participant(s) *and* for them to get to know you. Be open to discussions of daily life as you speak with each other about what brings you to the table.
- **Amistad**: From a place of reciprocity, begin to discuss the questions that, following the guidelines above in the "Interviews" section, together, you crafted. Where in interviews

you sometimes want to keep your words to a minimum, in a plática your goal is to have a dialogue—while you are interested in the experiences of the contributors, you too are a contributor to this conversation.

- **Despedida:** The farewell. To thank the participants for the conversation and their time, you may have brought them a small token of thanks, such as logo pens from your college. This is the time to offer them the gift. This is also the time where, as when having a conversation with family, things wind down and you move to say goodbye. As in an interview, you will remind contributors that you will be sending them a transcript of the conversation.

As you can see from the above steps, the plática is very similar to the Chicanx/Latinx interview. This is because the Chicanx/Latinx interview has been strongly influenced by Chicana feminist methodologies, and the plática *is* a Chicana feminist methodology. While respect for interviewees and participants is always part of our community's research methods, in the plática, reciprocity is central. Participants, including the facilitators, are "co-constructors of knowledge."[18] Because it is such a powerful Chicana feminist methodology, keeping in mind the basics of facilitating a plática will be useful for any type of interview you may conduct.

Testimonios

Testimonios are often categorized as a type of interview. In fact, the methodology for taking testimonios is similar to that for conducting interviews: the interviewer must do their homework and know the history and context of their subjects, they must develop their questions collaboratively, and they must establish a trust relationship with the speaker. They must check with their university regarding IRB review. With a testimonio, however, the politics of the questions and the context are explicit. As noted by Kathryn Blackmer Reyes and Julia Curry Rodríguez, "the testimonio is intentional and political."[19] As Dolores Delgado Bernal, Rebeca Burciaga, and Judith Flores Carmona explain in the introduction to that same volume:

> The *testimonio* challenges objectivity by situating the individual in communion with a collective experience marked by marginalization, oppression, or resistance. This approach has resulted in new understandings about how marginalized communities build solidarity and respond to and resist dominant culture, laws, and policies that perpetuate inequity.[20]

As you may have deduced, the testimonio, as a creative tool of resistance, flourished during the era of liberation movements, "in large part as a result of the liberation efforts and geopolitical resistance movements to imperialism in Third World nations."[21] Yet because testimonios are a tool for speaking back and challenging oppression, often the speaker takes great risks to speak back.

The roots of testimonios are in the Americas, especially revolutionary Latin America, where people spoke back to the violence and exploitation of regimes often supported by governments and moneyed interests abroad, including in the United States. As noted by Cinthya M. Saavedra, who uses testimonio as a teaching tool in her classrooms, testimonio "has been used by individuals to tell a collective story and history of oppression through the narrative of one individual."[22] The testimonio is necessarily collective, expressing the struggles, actions, and visions of a community through the voice of the speaker. Testimonios make visible "the political act of remembering."[23]

Normally the depth and amount of trust and reciprocity endemic to testimonios cannot be established in days or weeks.

Thus the use of testimonios for undergraduate scholars tends to be giving testimonio themselves in the context of a Chicanx or Latinx studies course, or using the transcript of a testimonio taken down by others in the context of completing a research project. As with interviews and pláticas, we must always be aware of our own social location when working with this critical material. We must also work with an awareness of the power of the words and the vulnerability of the speakers, including ourselves when we are the person speaking the testimonio. As noted by the mujeres of the Latina Feminist Group, speaking a testimonio is a process, one that includes reflecting on what can be said and what we choose not to share. It includes reflecting on the power of words to make ourselves and our communities stronger, but also to potentially make us more vulnerable.[24]

Because of the power of testimonios, college students are sometimes asked to work with them as part of learning about community resistance and the relationship of individuals to their community in times of oppression and of revolution. In working with their own testimonios, the Latina Feminist Group noted, "Testimonio is a complex genre that has multiple antecedents and uses." In naming the testimonios and antecedents that influence their work, they named the following powerful voices:

> Sojourner Truth, Jovita Idar, Anne Frank, Mercé Rodoreda, Rosario Castellanos, Julia de Burgos, Rigoberta Menchú, Adrienne Rich, Elena Poniatowska, Cherríe Moraga, Rosario Morales, Audre Lorde, Lorna Dee Cervantes, Isabel Allende, Toni Cade Bambara, Gioconda Belli, Ntozake Shange, Sara Estela Ramírez, Leslie Marmon Silko, Joy Harjo, Luci Tapahonso, Sandra Cisneros, and Gloria Anzaldúa.[25]

The testimonio of Domitila Barrios de Chungara, taken down by Moema Viezzer, is an example of this kind of powerful work. Barrios lived, labored, and organized in the mining towns of Bolivia in the latter half of the twentieth century. Daily struggle, family care, class struggle, and coming to concientización weave throughout her testimonio. Her testimonio is necessarily a collective story. Thus she names martyrs of the late twentieth-century Bolivian labor struggles: Federico Escobar Zapata, Rosendo García Maisman, and César Camacho. She writes of her coming to concientización, but also of the founding and work of the Housewives Committee. In relation, the actions of the repressive political regimes of her time against both herself and her community are central to the work: the massacres at Siglo XX, San Juan, and the Cochabamba Valley. She speaks of her own arrests and torture, of being kicked in the stomach until she lost her baby. She notes that when she was accused of being a communist, it made her investigate what communism was—it was then that she decided to become a communist.[26] The testimonio of Domitila Barrios de Chungara is an excellent example of the way in which testimonio weaves together the individual and communal, the personal and political, repression and resistance.

Concluding Thoughts

Chicanx and Latinx scholars share a long and rich tradition of interview, plática, and testimonio. This is because listening is central to the work that we do. Whether working with a written text or listening to a family member speak of their experiences, we do not assume objectivity but instead listen for voice, power, and perspective. When we conduct interviews or facilitate pláticas, we ask speakers to be vulnerable. Thus, all the basic reglas regarding respect and listening for Chicanx and Latinx research become exponentially important. While this powerful work can be intimidating, it is also rewarding. As noted by Vicki Ruiz in the opening of this chapter, "The consequences of oral history are lessons which the students and the instructor carry with them long after the [recording devices] are clicked off."

DISCUSSION QUESTIONS

1. Why are interviews critical to Chicanx and Latinx knowledge production?
2. What three kinds of questions are needed for most interviews?
3. Why are introductory questions important?
4. What is the Belmont Report and what does it teach us about scholarly research in the United States?
5. Why are scholars required to submit their research plans to IRBs before interviewing people?
6. What are some of the similarities between interviews, pláticas, and testimonios? What are some of the differences?
7. Have you read any of the testimonios named by the Latina Feminist Group? If so, what role did community play in the testimonio? What did the testimonio teach you about struggles for justice?
8. Think of a national or community event taking place in your lifetime. How did it change your understanding of yourself?

FURTHER READING

Deeb-Sossa, Natalia, and Louie F. Rodriguez, eds. *Community-Based Participatory Research: Testimonios from Chicana/o Studies.* Tucson: University of Arizona Press, 2019.

Delgado Bernal, Dolores, Rebeca Burciaga, and Judith Flores Carmona, eds. *Chicana/Latina Testimonios as Pedagogical, Methodological, and Activist Approaches to Social Justice.* London: Routledge, 2016.

García, Mario T., ed. *A Dolores Huerta Reader.* Albuquerque: University of New Mexico Press, 2008.

Ives, Edward D. *The Tape-Recorded Interview: A Manual for Fieldworkers in Folklore and Oral History.* 2nd ed. Knoxville: University of Tennessee Press, 1995.

Latina Feminist Group. *Telling to Live: Latina Feminist Testimonios.* Durham: Duke University Press, 2001.

Márquez, Lorena V. "Recovering Chicana/o Movement History Through Testimonios." In Deeb-Sossa and Rodríguez, *Community-Based Participatory Research*, 91–110.

Rubio-Goldsmith, Raquel. "Oral History: Considerations and Problems for Its Use in the History of Mexicanas." In *Between Borders: Essays on Mexicana/Chicana History*, edited by Adelaida R. Del Castillo, 161–73. Encino, Calif.: Floricanto Press, 1990.

Ruiz, Vicki L. "Situating Stories: The Surprising Consequences of Oral History." *Oral History Review* 25, no. 1–2 (Summer–Autumn 1998): 71–80. https://doi.org/10.1093/ohr/25.1.71.

Saavedra, Cinthya M. "Language and Literacy in the Borderlands: Acting upon the World Through 'Testimonios.'" *Language Arts* 88, no. 4 (2011): 261–69.

CHAPTER 5

How I Learned to Love Grammar and Forgive My Ninth-Grade English Teacher

I n this short chapter we provide explanations, with examples, of key tools for clear writing. For many of us, our exposure to grammatical rules was dry or confusing. Yet when we turn to texts by some of our favorite Chicanx and Latinx authors, we can see that one of the things that makes their work so powerful, and their arguments so convincing, is the strong grammatical structure they use. Below you will find information we have found helpful to share with undergraduates over the years. At the close of the chapter, we include a page of "Chicanx/Latinx Power Writing Rules." We recommend reviewing these writing rules each time you sit down to proof a paper.

The Basics: Sentences and Paragraphs
Sentence Structure

A complete sentence must have a subject (somebody or something that does something) and a predicate (a verb or action). In addition to this, a complete sentence must express a complete thought.

Examples:
1. Cherríe Moraga writes queer plays.
2. Lucha Corpi is a poet and a mystery author.
3. Iris Morales marched with the Young Lords.

Sound simple? Let us return to the last rule: a complete sentence must express a complete thought. This is where some students make mistakes in their writing. A sentence can have a subject and an action and still be incomplete. This is the case when you craft a dependent clause. When you begin a sentence with a word such as *since, because, when,* or *if,* you are opening your sentence with a dependent clause. Dependent clauses leave the reader waiting for more information.

When you open a sentence with a dependent clause, be sure to close the sentence with a short but complete sentence.

1. After the children finished choir practice, their teacher brought them out for paletas.
2. If a student graduates with a degree in ethnic studies, they will be prepared to solve real-world problems.
3. When you open a sentence with a dependent clause, be sure to close the sentence with an independent clause.

Notice how, in all of the above examples, the sentence fragment was made whole by adding a comma and an independent clause (short but complete sentence).

A Note About Paragraphs

Your paragraphs are the building blocks of your paper. If your bricks are weak, the building loses its strength and beauty. Yet it is absolutely counterproductive to proofread for cohesion as you write (***this would be an exercise in frustration***). Once you have completed your rough draft, edit your work to ensure that all paragraphs have strong topic sentences and that all information in the body of the paragraph supports or is related to the topic sentence.

Below find four cardinal rules for building strong paragraphs.

1. Every paragraph must have a strong topic sentence. The purpose of the topic sentence is to frame the information below it. Often the topic sentence will take a position on that information.
2. A topic sentence should not be more than two lines. Because the topic sentence frames the paragraph, a reader must be able to read it quickly and discern the significance of the paragraph.
3. All information in the body of a paragraph must support the topic sentence. Often when editing, you find that you included too much information in a paragraph. Slow down, break the paragraph into two or three paragraphs, and craft a topic sentence for each one.
4. Never begin a paragraph with a pronoun. Assume your reader is tired and overworked and will not remember the person or the event of which you are speaking.

Avoid These Evil Traps (Common Writing Errors)

Misplaced apostrophes: You should not use contractions in formal writing. Thus, do not write "It's," but instead "It is." Do not write "didn't," but instead "did not." In formal writing, edit out all contractions, then focus on using possessive apostrophes in their correct place.

For singular nouns, use an apostrophe followed by an *s*.
  Jorge's thesis
  Xiomara's novels
  Emma's discourse

For plural nouns, use an apostrophe but do NOT add an *s*.
  the professors' salaries
  the students' papers
  the artists' paintings

There are *very* few exceptions to this rule. For example, in those rare cases when a word ends in *s* in both its singular and plural form, add only an apostrophe to the end of the word.

> The clippers' blade was dull.
> The pajamas' button was missing.
> The headquarters' phone was out.

Again, these exceptions are rare; when first working with the possessive apostrophe, simply follow the basic rule.

Abrupt quotations: Always introduce a quotation (with just one or two lines). Who said it? Why is it important? This rule applies to both short and long (block) quotations.

Let Us Talk About Punctuation . . .
The Comma

There are many rules for comma usage. Below we address the four most common uses: to separate items in a list, to bracket off information in a sentence, to join an introductory phrase or clause to the rest of a sentence, and to join two independent clauses together with a conjunction.

SEPARATING ITEMS IN A LIST

This is one of the most common uses of the comma. Whenever you have a list of more than two items, use commas to separate the items. Often, grammar geeks will debate whether or not writers must use a comma if they use a conjunction before the last item. A comma used before the last item of a list with a conjunction such as *and* is called an Oxford comma. We believe that the Oxford comma helps a sentence read more smoothly, thus we recommend using it.

Examples:

1. Below we address the four most common uses: to separate items in a list, to bracket off information in a sentence, to join an introductory phrase or clause to the rest of a sentence, and to join two independent clauses together.

2. The figures of Reies López Tijerina, Rodolfo "Corky" Gonzales, José Angel Gutiérrez, and César Chávez have eclipsed a fuller historical understanding of these social movements, especially women's participation.[1]

3. Throughout her life Tenayuca kept abreast of worker-related issues, clipping newspaper articles, reading books, and helping young scholars interested in American labor history.[2]

Notice how, in each of the examples we provided, the writers use an Oxford comma.

BRACKETING OFF INFORMATION

Sometimes writers want to include details about a person or event without crafting another sentence for the information. This is where commas may be used to bracket the information off in what we call a "detail zone." The commas serve as brackets that hold the additional detail. The key to deciding if information should be bracketed with commas is to ask yourself if the sentence still makes sense when you remove the information.

Examples:

1. We believe that the Oxford comma helps a sentence read more smoothly, and "Oxford comma" sounds cool, thus we recommend using it.

2. The figure of La Llorona, although more prevalent in popular culture, does not always carry the same historical significance.[3]

3. As the main initiators of the First Mexicanist Congress, a
vehicle for the propagation of social change and cultural
redemption discourse, the Idar family embodied many of the
characteristics of México-Tejano middle-class reformers.[4]

JOINING AN INTRODUCTORY PHRASE OR CLAUSE TO THE REST OF A SENTENCE

Often we begin a sentence with an introductory phrase. Opening a sentence with an introductory phrase can help set the tone
or context for the sentence, but if you are not careful, this can
leave you with an incomplete sentence / sentence fragment. If
you begin a sentence with an introductory phrase, take extra
care to make sure your sentence is complete. The easiest way to
do this is to end the opening clause with a comma and to follow
the comma with an independent clause.

This is honestly and seriously not as complicated as it sounds.
Below find several examples of how to do this.

Examples:
1. Without these people, there would have been no movement.[5]
2. Although Mexican farm workers were the backbone of
the U.S. agricultural economy for some time, the Bracero
Program changed the way they were viewed by the larger
society.[6]
3. In the words of Gramsci (1971), their parents' experiences
"deposit" historical events and processes that influence how
the participants see the world around them.[7]

JOINING TWO INDEPENDENT CLAUSES

Often this is the one usage that students remember from their
ninth-grade English class. When you join two independent clauses
using a conjunction, a comma should precede the conjunction.
Note: if you are joining two independent clauses and ***not*** using
a conjunction, then you should use a semicolon.

Examples:

1. To Christians, who believe that moral conduct in life at least partially determines the nature of the afterlife, the Nahuatl view may seem strange, for there was no suggestion of punishment or reward in the hereafter.[8]

2. Martín-Baro suggests that the persistence of violence in society and the transmission of traumas persists beyond those who experienced them in El Salvador, and thus efforts to disclose these histories publicly and generationally are significant moves with the potential to transform societies in Central America and here in the United States.[9]

3. I look back and see a very impassioned me believing I had found my true self, and if there was nothing wrong with me, then it was the rules, the prejudice and the law that must be wrong, not others like me.[10]

The Semicolon

There are three main uses for the semicolon: joining two independent clauses, joining two independent clauses with a conjunctive adverb (adverbs that join parts of sentences), and listing things.

JOINING TWO INDEPENDENT CLAUSES

The semicolon is a wonderful tool for connecting two closely related sentences or independent clauses. Below find several examples from the work of well-known Chicanx and Latinx scholars. Always make sure that both sides of your semicolon can stand on their own.

Examples:

1. My Grandmother Salcido reflected on the aftermath of her mother's decision to marry a mestizo, out of love; the outcome of this decision was why she is now buried alongside

the remains of those whom she chose to adopt as her family, as her relations.[11]

2. Separated from Mexico, the Native Mexican-Texan no longer looked toward Mexico as home; the Southwest became our homeland once more.[12]

3. I drove home confounded by happiness and yearning; I had never felt this for anyone.[13]

Notice how, in each of the above sentences, both clauses are complete; they can stand alone. At the same time, the ideas or facts they express are very closely related.

JOINING TWO INDEPENDENT CLAUSES WITH A CONJUNCTIVE ADVERB

A semicolon should also be used when you join two complete clauses with a conjunctive adverb such as *however, nonetheless, thus,* or *therefore.*

Remember, while an adverb modifies a verb, a conjunctive adverb's function is to join two complete phrases (hence the *junct,* meaning "join," in *conjunctive*).

Common Conjunctive Adverbs (keeping the *junct* in conjunctive adverbs):	
additionally	nevertheless
also	next
certainly	nonetheless
finally	now
furthermore	otherwise
hence	regardless
however	still
in addition	then
instead	therefore
likewise	thus
meanwhile	yet

Here are two examples of semicolons used in this fashion.

1. The Teutonics did not question the earlier romantic historians' interpretation of continental expansion as God-
   ordained manifest destiny; instead, they recast the same
   view in terms of evolutionary theory.[14]
2. Padilla agrees that the arts are important in being able to
   communicate messages and provide information; however,
   she does suggest a question that may need further investigation. How does all of this exposure to the arts actually
   manifest into action, and how can this be measured?[15]

Note how the semicolon joins two complete clauses and that *the
second clause begins with a conjunctive adverb.*

LISTS, LISTS, LISTS

When writing essays, a list can be introduced with a colon, with
each item followed by a comma. But what happens when you
need to include some detail about the items in your list? That is
when it becomes necessary to use semicolons.

Examples:

1. It [*blu*] received additional support from the Playwrights'
   Center's Jerome Fellowship, the Enye Project, the Ellen
   Stone Belic Institute for the Student of Women and Gender
   in the Arts and the Media, Austin Script Works' Head 2
   Head Program, and the following series of staged readings:
   Los Angeles Theatre Centre, directed by Maureen Hus-
   key; Victory Gardens Theatre in Chicago, IL, directed by
   Daniel Janquez; Alliance Theatre in Atlanta, GA, directed by
   Susan Reid; New York Theatre Workshop in New York City,
   directed by Carl Hancock Rux; and the Vortex Theatre in
   Austin Texas, directed by Florinda Bryant.[16]
2. By reading the printed *brindis* as a trace of the original
   vocal and performative gesture, this article asserts that

the verses of these women were a three-fold protest: first,
through their performance in the public sphere, these Latinas disrupted their political disenfranchisement as women;
second, they contested outright European tyrants; and
third, by verbalizing anti-colonial sentiments more broadly,
they protested their annexation by the U.S. in a shrouded,
but powerful way.[17]

Note that a colon marks the spot where each list begins. Within
each list the semicolon allows the author to include details about
the items they list. For complicated lists, where you need to include detailed information, the semicolon is your friend.

The Power of Writing

Of course, many more important tips for clear and fabulous writing exist. The next two pages consist of what we call "Chicanx/
Latinx Power Writing Rules." This is the sheet with which we
begin any course in which our students will have to write a research paper or essay. We recommend that you read over this
sheet every time you have a writing assignment, and that you
utilize it as a "cheat sheet" to proof your papers. Also, two sites
that we find useful whenever we need our own writing questions
answered are:

> OWL, Purdue University Writing Lab, https://owl.purdue.edu
> /owl/purdue_owl.html.
> Writing Center, Walden University, https://academicguides
> .waldenu.edu/writingcenter.

Chicanx/Latinx Power Writing Rules

Structure:
1. Always save your document with your name in the file name
   and on the paper. Always back up your work.

2. Have a clear thesis statement you can successfully defend throughout the body of your paper.
3. Be self-conscious about the organization of your paragraphs. Make sure that each paragraph has a topic sentence, evidence, and analysis connecting the evidence to the paragraph's main argument. Formal essays never use one-sentence paragraphs! THIS IS CRITICAL. Paragraphs should not be too long or short. Craft transitions to bring your reader from one paragraph (building block) to the next.
4. When using quotations, introduce them and discuss them. They must read as critical and integral parts of your argument. With Chicago formatting, long quotations must be indented one half inch on both sides and single-spaced. With MLA formatting, long quotations must be indented one half inch from the left margin and should remain double-spaced.
5. Craft a strong conclusion that reminds readers of why your topic and your findings are important.

Rules:
1. In general, be selective with the use of the second and the first person in your paper. While it is important to place yourself in relation to your topic, you should not use phrases such as "I think" as part of your argument (instead, state your evidence).
2. Avoid casual or colloquial speech ("got," "huge," etc.). That is, do not write the way you speak. For example, ending a sentence with a preposition is fine in spoken English, but not in written English. Use formal, professional language (reading journals such as *Aztlán* and *Chicana/Latina Studies* will help you develop this tone). Do not use contractions.
3. Avoid summarizing and using sweeping generalizations. In other words, do not begin an essay with such statements as "History shows us that . . ." or "People have always . . ."

4. Avoid using adverbs like "horribly," "incredibly," or "terribly," or empty modifiers like "very."

5. Never refer to a writer or a historical figure by their first name alone. Use their full name the first time mentioned and then use only their last name(s). Make sure you copy their name(s) correctly and respect their use of accents, ñ, and other characters not used in English.

6. When you begin writing, decide which verb tense is most appropriate for your paper and be consistent.

7. Write in active voice, not passive voice. Because we want to describe our people as actors with agency, "Lupe stressed the importance of proofreading" is better than "The importance of proofreading was stressed by Lupe." Using passive voice with people renders them as objects and displaces the responsibility of the actors. For instance, "Mexican immigrants were discriminated against" leaves out crucial information about who performed this discrimination, treating it as if it were a neutral fact. Instead, we assign the blame/responsibility where it belongs: "Euro-Americans from the Happy Valley suburb discriminated against Mexican immigrants."

8. Never begin a paragraph with a pronoun. Even if you believe your reader will know the person or place about which you are writing, use the proper name for your subject.

9. Use your thesaurus. Some word processing programs have a drop-down menu for this task. Locate synonyms for words that appear frequently in the essay. Avoid repeating a word multiple times in one paragraph.

When you are (almost) finished:

1. Double-check your list of basics. Did you remember:
   - ✓ A creative title and subtitle?
   - ✓ Page numbers?
   - ✓ Double spacing?

✓ Indented block quotations (indented with single spacing for history papers)?

✓ Citations for all sources and a bibliography or works-cited page?

2. Check for consistency between your thesis and your conclusion.

3. Leave yourself enough time to proofread (read your work aloud) and edit your paper before handing it in.

The Art of Citation

Chicago Footnotes/Endnotes and Bibliographies

For any work that we produce, we must attribute the facts and ideas we use to our sources.[1] Citations credit authors for their work and help our readers discover sources that are important in the field. As discussed in chapter 2, when you begin a new research project, looking at a book's or an article's footnotes or endnotes and bibliography can provide you with leads and sources for your project. Your citations, footnotes/endnotes, and bibliography can help your readers do the same.

For historians, as in a growing number of other fields, Chicago citations are the preferred citation style because they contain all the critical detail a reader needs to quickly locate a source. Last year, for example, I wrote an article about Dolores Huerta for an anthology about Catholic women's rhetoric. The anthology was firmly rooted in the field of rhetoric, not history, but the publisher required that all authors use Chicago citations.

For your generation, Chicago citations are relatively easy to incorporate into your work because word processing software includes everything you need to create your footnotes/endnotes. When you choose "Reference" from your toolbar, and then "Insert Footnote" (References → Insert Footnote), the software brings you directly to where you must key in your information; it then tracks your entries, *and*, if you add information at a later date, it automatically renumbers your notes.

Below you will find citation examples, following the *Chicago Manual of Style*'s 17th edition, for the types of sources college students most frequently use. This is followed by a resource list for learning more about Chicago citations, and finally a student paper on Chicana history demonstrating how one student utilized Chicago footnotes in a rich and informative manner. Over the years I have come to love the rich detail of Chicago citations, and I hope that you will too.

Footnotes/Endnotes and Bibliography Entries for Common Sources

Footnotes/endnotes (hereafter simply called notes): Notes must be numbered and should include page numbers whenever possible. Remember, when you choose "References" and then "Footnote" (or "Endnote") from your toolbar, it numbers your notes for you. Book, journal, and magazine titles are always italicized; article titles are always placed within quotation marks. For each title, use title case (the capitalization used for books). Do not capitalize entire words; instead, capitalize the first letter of every significant word (do not capitalize articles or coordinating conjunctions such as *and* or *or*).

After you include the full information for a source, you can use a *shortened* or *concise* note thereafter. A shortened note includes the author's last name, followed by a comma, a shortened title, another comma, then the pages utilized.

Bibliography entries: Bibliography entries contain much of the same information as notes, but with some important differences. In a bibliography you must list the last name of the author first. This helps your reader navigate their way through your list of sources and locate specific authors quickly and easily. Next, some of the punctuation in bibliography entries is slightly different from the punctuation in notes (periods where there were once commas, no parentheses). Finally, with article and book chapter entries you must include the page numbers for the full article or chapter, not just the pages utilized. Initially this may seem complicated, but it will become less difficult with practice.

Books
SINGLE-AUTHOR BOOKS
Note Format:
Author's First and Last Name, *Book Title* (Place of Publication: Publisher, year), page number(s) utilized.

Bibliography Format:
Author's Last Name, First Name. *Book Title*. Place of Publication: Publisher, year.

Note Examples (First Use):
Catrióna Rueda Esquibel, *With Her Machete in Her Hand: Reading Chicana Lesbians* (Austin: University of Texas Press, 2006), 23–34.
Alicia Gaspar de Alba, *[Un]framing the "Bad Woman": Sor Juana, Malinche, Coyolxauhqui and Other Rebels with a Cause* (Austin: University of Texas Press, 2014), 2.

Shortened/Concise:
Esquibel, *With Her Machete*, 23–34.
Gaspar de Alba, *[Un]framing*, 2.

Bibliography Examples:
Esquibel, Catrióna Rueda. *With Her Machete in Her Hand: Reading Chicana Lesbians*. Austin: University of Texas Press, 2006.
Gaspar de Alba, Alicia. *[Un]framing the "Bad Woman": Sor Juana, Malinche, Coyolxauhqui and Other Rebels with a Cause*. Austin: University of Texas Press, 2014.

BOOKS IN A LATER EDITION
Note Example:
Rodolfo Acuña, *Occupied America: A History of Chicanos*, 3rd ed. (New York: Harper Collins, 1988), 56–70.

Shortened/Concise:
Acuña, *Occupied America*, 56–70.

Note how, even for later editions, your shortened/concise note references only need to include the author's last name, shortened title, and page number(s) utilized.

Bibliography Example:
Acuña, Rodolfo. *Occupied America: A History of Chicanos*. 3rd ed. New York: Harper Collins, 1988.

Book Chapters
SINGLE CHAPTER FROM AN EDITED ANTHOLOGY/COLLECTION
If using a chapter from an edited anthology, you must include the name of the editor(s) and the title of the anthology as well as the author's name and chapter title.

Note Format:
Author's First and Last Name, "Title of Chapter," in *Title of Anthology*, ed. Editor's First and Last Name (Place of Publication: Publisher, year), page numbers.

Note Examples:
Gloria Anzaldúa, "To(o) Queer the Writer—Loca, escritora y chicana," in *Living Chicana Theory*, ed. Carla Trujillo (Berkeley: Third Woman Press, 1997), 263–68.
Nan Alamilla Boyd, "Bodies in Motion: Lesbian and Transsexual Histories," in *The Transgender Studies Reader*, ed. Susan Stryker and Stephen Whittle (New York: Routledge, 2006), 425.

Bibliography Examples:

For a chapter from an anthology, the formatting is very similar to that of a basic book entry, but you must include the name of the editor(s) and the page numbers of the chapter. This information precedes the publishing information.

Anzaldúa, Gloria. "To(o) Queer the Writer—Loca, escritora y chicana." In *Living Chicana Theory*, edited by Carla Trujillo, 263–76. Berkeley: Third Woman Press, 1997.

Boyd, Nan Alamilla. "Bodies in Motion: Lesbian and Transsexual Histories." In *The Transgender Studies Reader*, edited by Susan Stryker and Stephen Whittle, 420–33. New York: Routledge, 2006.

Periodicals
JOURNAL ARTICLES

Note Format:

Author's First and Last Name, "Title and Subtitle of Article," *Journal Name* volume number, issue number (Date): page numbers utilized. If the article is electronic, the URL or DOI follows the page numbers after a comma.

Note Examples:

Francisco J. Galarte, "On Trans* Chican@s: Amor, Justicia, y Dignidad," *Aztlán* 39, no. 1 (Spring 2014): 233.

Francisco Valdez, "'We Are Now of the View': Backlash Activism, Cultural Cleansing, and the Kulturkampf to Resurrect the Old Deal," *Seton Hall Law Review* 35, no. 4 (2005): 1448–49.

Bibliography Format:

As for book entries, the format is very similar to that of its corresponding note. Where there were once commas, there are now periods. Where in the note you cited only the pages utilized, in the bibliography you must cite the full page range for the article.

Author's Last Name, First Name. "Title and Subtitle of Article." *Journal Name* volume number, issue number (Date): pages.

Bibliography Examples:
Galarte, Francisco J. "On Trans* Chican@s: Amor, Justicia, y Dignidad."
 Aztlán 39, no. 1 (Spring 2014): 229–36.
Valdez, Francisco. "'We Are Now of the View': Backlash Activism, Cultural Cleansing, and the Kulturkampf to Resurrect the Old Deal."
 Seton Hall Law Review 35, no. 4 (2005): 1407–63.

NEWSPAPER AND MAGAZINE ARTICLES
Note: If no author is listed, begin your entry with the article title.
As with journal articles, if a source is an online source, you must
also include its URL.

Note Format:
Author's First and Last Name, "Title and Subtitle of Article," *Name of
 Newspaper or Magazine*, Date of Publication, page number(s).

Note Examples:
"Grand Jury Report," *Napa Register*, September 12, 1863, 1.
"Male-Clad Girl at the Lake," *Stockton Evening Mail*, August 27, 1897, 1.

Bibliography:
Normally, individual newspaper articles are not listed in the bibliography. Instead, you will list the newspaper and the range of
years utilized in your research. If located at an archive, you will
also list the archive.

Napa Register, 1861–1869.
Stockton Evening Mail, 1897–1898.

Interviews
ORIGINAL INTERVIEW
Note Format:
First and Last Name of Interviewee, the phrase "interview by author,"
 type of record, Place of Interview, Date of Interview.

Note Example:
Earl Couey, interview by author, tape recording, Napa, CA, August 28, 1998.

Bibliography Example:
Couey, Earl. Interview with author. Napa, CA. August 28, 1998.

PUBLISHED INTERVIEW
Note Format:
First and Last Name of Interviewee, "Title of Interview," by First and Last Name of Interviewer, *Journal Title* volume number, issue number (Date): page(s) utilized.

Note Example:
Ruby Bracamonte, "'My Story Is Really Not Mine': An Interview with Latina Trans Activist Ruby Bracamonte," by Sharon Doetsch Kidder, *Feminist Studies* 37, no. 2 (2011): 452, http://www.jstor.org/stable /23069913.

Bibliography Format:
As with journal articles, there are slight differences between an interview citation in a note and its entry in the bibliography.

Interviewee Last Name, First Name. "Title and Subtitle." By Interviewer First and Last Name. *Journal Title* volume number, issue number (Date): page range.

Bibliography Example:
Bracamonte, Ruby. "'My Story Is Really Not Mine': An Interview with Latina Trans Activist Ruby Bracamonte." By Sharon Doetsch-Kidder. *Feminist Studies* 37, no. 2 (2011): 441–67. http://www.jstor.org/stable /23069913.

Yet Another Note About Bibliographies

References in your bibliography should *not* be numbered. Instead, list your sources in alphabetical order, last name first. When there is no name, list alphabetically by document name.

FURTHER READING AND RESOURCES

Chicago Manual of Style Quick Guide: While there is a fee to access the full *Chicago Manual of Style*, the press makes their quick guide free to the public. https://www.chicagomanualofstyle.org/tools_citation guide/citation-guide-1.html.

Owl Purdue: The Writing Lab at Purdue University has one of the most comprehensive reference guides for using Chicago-style citations. https://owl.purdue.edu/owl/research_and_citation/chicago_manual _17th_edition/cmos_formatting_and_style_guide/chicago_manual _of_style_17th_edition.html.

Sample Student History Paper

Take note of the formatting the student, César E. Castañeda, uses throughout the paper. There is a title page with the title centered and in title case, and the student's name and the course name below (about a third of a page from the bottom). The body of the paper is double-spaced with no extra spaces between paragraphs. All notes are single-spaced with a space between each note. Also notice that the student's longer quotations (those longer than four lines) are indented and single-spaced.

The Legacy of a Guerrera:
Anna NietoGomez

César E. Castañeda

WST 454: La Chicana in U.S. Society

Washington State University, Pullman

April 4, 2018

1

 In its early years, the movement working for the advancement of Chicanas/os in the United States, the Chicano Movement, did not engage a feminist lens. That is to say, the Chicano Movement functioned in a male-centric manner. To combat this, many Chicanas had to push for equality within the movement—to fight for a movement that did not place the needs of one group above the needs of another. Because the Chicano Movement was a national movement, addressing a vast number of issues, working for equality within the movement was a complex undertaking involving many people. Anna NietoGomez, a strong Xicanista, was one of these people; she stood up for her fellow Chicanas and she created a space for future generations to live and thrive in. In order to understand the impact of Anna NietoGomez, it is first vital to understand why there was a need for such activism.

 While the Chicano Movement was and is very important, it was also flawed. The movement, as described by José Ángel Gutiérrez, was "a social movement that occurred in the United States with increased activity in the Southwest and Midwest during a time frame: 1950s to 1980s. Persons of Mexican ancestry residing in the U.S. were its participants and self-identified as Chicanos."[1] It is imperative to note that self-identified Chicanos fought not only to empower themselves but also to challenge the government. This included how they named themselves. They fought police harassment, worked for labor rights, fought racism in the schools and discrimination in the workplace, and named themselves Chicano.[2] They chose a name for themselves that expressed pride in their history and in their working-class heritage. "Chicano," they said, came from the Mexicas, the people who ruled Mexico before the Europeans came.[3]

---

 1. José Ángel Gutiérrez, "The Chicano Movement: Paths to Power," *Social Studies* 102, no. 1 (2010): 25, https://doi.org/10.1080/00377996.2011.533043.

 2. Gutiérrez, "Chicano Movement," 26–29.

 3. Gutiérrez, "Chicano Movement," 25; Elizabeth Martínez, *De Colores Means All of Us: Latina Views for a Multi-colored Century* (Cambridge, MA: South End Press, 1988), 2.

2

While the Chicano Movement had the end goal of "the acquisition of political power with which to change the power relations between themselves and Euro-Americans," it did so in a sexist way.[4] It ignored issues that the women in its communities raised, such as gender discrimination in labor and politics, inequality in the family, and reproductive rights. Male leaders in the Chicano Movement told women that they would return later to the topics that affected women, since it would be easier to do so once they had achieved their initial goals. This is where Chicanas stepped in to push the movement to become intersectional, to address all issues as they intersected with gender. Doing this meant addressing job discrimination against Chicanos and Chicanas. It meant addressing job discrimination in college campus clubs. It meant addressing health and reproductive health.[5]

When the men in the movement ignored women's issues, they ignored the fact that strong and feminist women have a deep history in our communities. Sor Juana Inés de la Cruz, a seventeenth-century nun, criticized the double standard.[6] The club Las Hijas de Cuauhtémoc worked for women's right to vote, and Emma Tenayuca, Josefina Fierro de Bright, and Luisa Moreno fought for civil rights and worker rights in the 1920s and '30s.[7] The UFW, where so many college students volunteered, was co-founded by Dolores Huerta.[8] Yet once the Chicano Movement began to take shape, many organizations, especially college organizations, forgot about this history. One of the ways that the Chicanas of the 1970s would fight for women's rights was by reminding our

4. Gutiérrez, "Chicano Movement," 25–32.

5. "Chicanas Attend Vancouver Conference," in *Chicana Feminist Thought: The Basic Historical Writings*, ed. Alma M. García (New York: Routledge, 1997), 151 (originally published in *La Verdad*, no. 28, May 1971); Francisca Flores, "Comisión Femenil Mexicana," in García, *Chicana Feminist Thought*, 150 (originally published in *Regeneración* 2, no. 1 [1971]: 6–7).

6. Martínez, De Colores, 163.

7. Vicki Ruiz, *From Out of the Shadows: Mexican Women in Twentieth-Century America* (New York: Oxford University Press, 2008), 72–98; Maylei Blackwell, *¡Chicana Power! Contested Histories of Feminism in the Chicano Movement* (Austin: University of Texas Press, 2016), 48–49.

8. Alicia Chávez, "Dolores Huerta and the United Farm Workers," in *Latina Legacies: Identity, Biography, and Community*, ed. Vicki L. Ruiz and Virginia Sánchez Korrol (New York: Oxford University Press, 2005), 240–54.

3

communities of this history. The women of one of the organizations that NietoGomez helped to

found named themselves Las Hijas de Cuauhtémoc.

Anna NietoGomez was born in San Bernardino, California, in 1946 to a mother that worked

for the Santa Fe Railroad and a World War II veteran father. She was a third-generation Chicana

with roots in New Mexico dating back to the 1600s.[9] What is interesting about NietoGomez is how

keenly aware she was of sexism and other forms of discrimination, not only in her own community

but also in her very own home. NietoGomez remembered "that growing up in a segregated

community made her aware of racism from an early age."[10] In an interview with Maylei Blackwell,

NietoGomez told of an experience of sexism in her own home, telling the historian:

> Another important thing to me was that my grandma did not eat at the same table as
> my grandpa. He ate by himself like a patrón, and for whatever reason, I don't know
> where I got it, I thought that it was wrong. She would cook dinner or breakfast or
> lunch, and we were allowed to eat at the same table as my grandpa, but my grandma
> would not eat at that table until everyone was finished—like a servant, like she wasn't
> family—so that didn't seem right to me since neither my father nor my other
> grandfather treated their wives this way.[11]

NietoGomez noted that, even as a young girl, she saw sexism and she challenged sexism. In this case,

she did something about it through a small hunger strike. When her grandfather insisted that her

grandmother did not need to join them, NietoGomez told him she would not eat until her

grandmother ate with the whole family. Her grandfather relented and called NietoGomez's

grandmother to the table, and they ate together thereafter.[12]

This small act of revolution had the potential for a larger impact, especially for the future. In

telling her history to Maylei Blackwell, NietoGomez created a testimonio. A testimonio is a

---

9. Blackwell, *¡Chicana Power!*, 50–52.

10. Ramiro Alvarez, "Anna Nieto-Gomez," Chicana Por Mi Raza, accessed May 1, 2018,
http://chicanapormiraza.org/chicanas/anna-nieto-gomez.

11. Blackwell, *¡Chicana Power!*, 51.

12. Blackwell, *¡Chicana Power!*, 51.

4

narrative given by an eyewitness with the purpose of drawing attention to an oppressive situation, politicizing their experience in order to challenge cultural and/or societal inequalities.[13] In this situation, by not only drawing attention to her grandfather's behavior but also framing it in a way that demonstrated the sexist, machista nature of his actions, NietoGomez challenged this sexist behavior in families and in homes. NietoGomez promoted a model of fighting back in a person's own home, moving toward a society in which sexism no longer exists. NietoGomez left this story for the Chicanistas in future generations to take inspiration from, teaching them that it is possible to have a voice in society while simultaneously empowering them to believe in themselves as Chicanas.

Anna NietoGomez went on to attend California State University Long Beach (at the time Long Beach State College) in 1967, and quickly became involved in activism on campus. As is the case at many universities today, in the 1960s institutes of higher education were oppressive settings; Chicano and Chicana students were surrounded by white students, faculty, staff, and culture. In the 1970s the environment was even more Eurocentric than today. The curriculum did not include Chicano or Latino studies, there was no Chicanx/Latinx student union, and many professors did not try to address their own racism. Chicano/a students, in order to survive, organized. While NietoGomez was still a student at Cal State Long Beach, she and J. Anthony Vasquez prepared a study on the needs of Chicano university students and found that, "of the two per cent of Spanish surname students in college, only one-half of one per cent ever receive their degree."[14] The racism she and other Chicanas and Chicanos experienced pushed her to become involved in El Movimiento Estudiantil Chicano de Aztlán (MEChA).[15]

---

13. Latina Feminist Group, *Telling to Live: Latina Feminist Testimonios* (Durham: Duke University Press, 2002), 13.

14. Anna NietoGomez and J. Anthony Vasquez, "The Needs of the Chicano on the College Campus" (paper presented at the Conference on Increasing Opportunities for Mexican American Students in Higher Education, California State College, Long Beach, May 1969), https://eric.ed.gov/?id=ED031323.

15. Alvarez, "Anna Nieto-Gomez."

5

It was in MEChA that NietoGomez was elected democratically to the position of president of the club. What began as an important win in her life soon turned into a nightmare. NietoGomez was verbally harassed and even was hung in effigy by MEChA members. Historian Maylei Blackwell notes, "They held a procession and mock burial for Chicana student movement leaders where coffins were placed in front of tombstones with the names Anna NietoGomez, Corinne Sánchez, and Norma Owens on them."[16] This was an unsettling display, demonstrating that even within spaces created for Chicanas/os there was overt sexism and machismo. The harassment of Chicanas who dared to take leadership roles was a factor for NietoGomez, along with Corinne Sánchez and others, to create a Xicanista group for themselves, Las Hijas De Cuauhtémoc.

Hijas de Cuauhtémoc was an intersectional club for students who faced racism and sexism. This club created a space for Xicanas to collaborate and empower themselves and each other. One such result of this collaboration was a new journal developed to explore what it meant to be a Chicana and to address issues that affected them as Chicanas—a publication named *Encuentro Femenil*. In one issue of the journal NietoGomez addressed a Chicana's experience with discrimination and political positions, explaining the importance of the needs of Chicanas as Chicanas, writing:

> The Chicana's socio-economic class as a non-Anglo, Spanish-speaking, low-income Chicana woman determines her need and therefore her political position. The low-income Anglo woman does not have to deal with racism nor is she punished because she speaks another language. The middle-class Anglo woman only shares with the Chicana the fact that they are both women. But they are women of different ethnic, cultural, and class status. All these factors determine the different socio-economic needs and therefore determine the different political positions of these women.[17]

NietoGomez was not afraid to directly address the issues that surround Xicanistas, in this case the differences between Anglo women and women of color—brown women. She pushed readers of

---

16. Blackwell, *¡Chicana Power!*, 80.

17. Anna NietoGomez, "La Femenista," in García, *Chicana Feminist Thought*, 90–91. This article was originally published in *Encuentro Femenil* 1, no. 2 (1974): 34–47.

6

Encuentro Femenil to use an intersectional analysis that used race, class, *and* gender to understand the challenges of Chicanas in US society.

It is important to address the fact that even after NietoGomez and other Chicanas founded organizations such as Las Hijas de Cuauhtémoc, they continued to confront sexism within the Chicano Movement and within society. Surprisingly, there was even resistance against these organizations by Chicanas. As historian Vicki Ruiz notes, "Some coeds proved reluctant to join campus Chicana organizations, like Hijas de Cuauhtémoc at Cal State, Long Beach, for fear of being labeled or rejected by men."[18] Some women were hesitant to speak out against the discrepancies and oppression they faced based on their ethnicities and gender. This was not an isolated event at CSU Long Beach. Several years after her work as a student at Long Beach, NietoGomez went on to write the film *CHICANA*, which critiqued the complacent attitude that some women still held in the 1970s. As described by Perlita Dicochea, the film "opens with scenes that depict the domestic lifestyles that many women accepted without question. . . . 'We free men to work,' says the female voice over. 'We prepare the future labor force.'"[19] Long after she graduated from Long Beach, Anna NietoGomez continued to call Chicanas to action and to move our communities forward.

Anna NietoGomez is perhaps one of the greatest Xicanistas of her era, leaving a lasting impact not only in Long Beach, California, but in the larger Chicano movement. At a young age she began fighting the sexism in her own home, the machismo that normalized her grandfather's treatment of her grandmother. In college she helped found Las Hijas de Cuauhtémoc, an organization to serve the needs of Chicanas. She served as president of MEChA when few Chicanas—in fact, few women—held public leadership roles on campus. She wrote articles, and went

---

18. Ruiz, *From Out of the Shadows*, 108.

19. Perlita R. Dicochea, "Chicana Critical Rhetoric: Recrafting La Causa in Chicana Movement Discourse, 1970–1979," *Frontiers: A Journal of Women Studies* 25, no. 1 (2004): 81.

7

on to write a movie and to create some of the first academic courses in Chicana studies. She helped found an organization that opened a space to address the problems facing Chicanas openly and without fear of backlash. NietoGomez was an inspiration to Chicana activists in the twentieth century and she continues her activism with speeches today, passing down her wisdom and experiences even as an elder. Her history of activism will inspire Chicanas and Chicanos for generations to come.

8

Bibliography

Alvarez, Ramiro. "Anna Nieto-Gomez." Chicana Por Mi Raza. Accessed May 1, 2018.
http://chicanapormiraza.org/chicanas/anna-nieto-gomez.

Blackwell, Maylei. ¡Chicana Power! Contested Histories of Feminism in the Chicano Movement.
Austin: University of Texas Press, 2016.

Chávez, Alicia. "Dolores Huerta and the United Farm Workers." In Latina Legacies: Identity,
Biography, and Community, edited by Vicki L. Ruiz and Virginia Sánchez Korrol, 240–54.
New York: Oxford University Press, 2005.

"Chicanas Attend Vancouver Conference." In Chicana Feminist Thought: The Basic Historical
Writings, edited by Alma M. García, 151–52. New York: Routledge, 1997.

"Defining Chicana Feminisms: In Their Own Words." Making Face, Making Soul: A Chicana
Feminist Homepage. Accessed February 9, 2018. http://www.chicanas.com/defs.htm#nieto.

Dicochea, Perlita R. "Chicana Critical Rhetoric: Recrafting La Causa in Chicana Movement
Discourse, 1970–1979." Frontiers 25, no. 1 (2004): 77–92.

Flores, Francisca. "Comisión Femenil Mexicana." In Chicana Feminist Thought: The Basic
Historical Writings, edited by Alma M. García, 150. New York: Routledge, 1997.

Gutiérrez, José Ángel. "The Chicano Movement: Paths to Power." Social Studies 102, no. 1 (2010):
25–32. https://doi.org/10.1080/00377996.2011.533043.

Latina Feminist Group. Telling to Live: Latina Feminist Testimonios. Durham: Duke University
Press, 2002.

Martínez, Elizabeth. De Colores Means All of Us: Latina Views for a Multi-colored Century.
Cambridge, MA: South End Press, 1998.

NietoGomez, Anna. "La Feminista." In Chicana Feminist Thought: The Basic Historical Writings,
edited by Alma M. García, 86–92. New York: Routledge, 1997.

NietoGomez, Anna, and J. Anthony Vasquez. "The Needs of the Chicano on the College Campus."
Paper presented at the Conference on Increasing Opportunities for Mexican American
Students in Higher Education, California State College, Long Beach, May 1969.
https://eric.ed.gov/?id=ED031323.

Ruiz, Vicki L. From Out of the Shadows: Mexican Women in Twentieth-Century America. New York:
Oxford University Press, 2008.

Ruiz, Vicki L., and Virginia Sánchez Korrol. Latinas in the United States: A Historical Encyclopedia.
Bloomington: Indiana University Press, 2006.

APPENDIX C

The Art of Citation

Modern Language Association (MLA) In-Text
Citations and Works Cited

When you write an essay on Chicanx and Latinx literature or culture, your professor will require you to use in-text citations (for the sources you quote or paraphrase), footnotes or endnotes, and a works-cited list where readers can easily find all pertinent information leading them to the sources you cited in your writing.[1] As discussed in chapter 3, the bibliographic citations from the sources we find for our own essay are useful to help us find additional materials about our topic(s). Therefore, when you produce your own writing, and your own works-cited list, you are also contributing to the list of sources that your readers can use for their work.

For those of us in the fields of Chicanx and Latinx literature and culture, the *MLA Handbook* produced by the Modern Language Association is the preferred guide for citing sources. A number of online publications can help you determine the exact way in which you cite a source depending on its format (an article in an anthology or an encyclopedia, a film, a chapter in a book, or a book). MLA style uses notes only when it is necessary to provide additional information that does not fit in the body of the essay. To give credit to the authors and artists whose work you are quoting, referencing, or paraphrasing, this style uses what we call in-text citations. These in-text citations are placed between parentheses in the main text; they generally include the author's or authors' last name(s), followed by the page number from the work where the quotation or information is found. There is no need to use a comma or other punctuation between these two pieces of information. You will see examples and details below, all following the ninth edition of the *MLA Handbook* (or MLA 9).

Each of the in-text citations should match an entry in the works-cited list at the end of your essay. The works-cited list is essentially a bibliography, with one important characteristic: It should include all of the works you cite, paraphrase, or reference substantially, and only those works. It should not include works that you do not use directly in your paper, even if they seem relevant to you or if you read them in preparation for writing your essay. In the works-cited list, full bibliographic information is given for all sources to help your readers locate them. In this book, chapter 3 is written in MLA style utilizing in-text citations, and it offers a works-cited list; it provides many examples of how to use notes and how to organize bibliographic information in a formal essay.

Although notes are few in MLA style, if you do include footnotes or endnotes, your word processing program should easily help you incorporate them into your essay. In MS Word, for instance, under the tab titled "References," there is a section that has the letters AB with a red number 1 above it. Below this image, in small letters, it says "Insert Footnote," and next to that section is the "Insert Endnote" button (References → Insert Footnote, or References → Endnote). The program will automatically number the notes when you insert or delete them. If you decide that you must add a note in the middle of a sentence, whenever possible, place it right after a punctuation mark (like a comma or semicolon), but never after a dash. In the note itself, leave one single space between the number and the first word of your note. Avoid adding too many details to your endnotes; instead, think of this space as the part of your essay where you will include important information that you believe your reader should know, but which should not interrupt the flow of your sentence or paragraph. If you decide that it is necessary to add a quotation or paraphrased ideas from your sources into your notes, you will need to cite them with in-text citations as you do in the main text of your essay.

This appendix includes examples of the types of sources most commonly used by college students and a list of resources for learning more about MLA citations. Appendix D includes a sample essay by Zabdi J. Salazar, who wrote it at the end of her first semester at Trinity University in San Antonio, Texas. She won the university-wide award when she submitted it to the first-year student writing competition. Her essay illustrates how the MLA style of citation is used and how an MLA-style works-cited section is organized.

In-Text Citations and Works-Cited Entries for Common Sources

Whenever you reference, quote, or paraphrase a text that you consider important evidence for your argument or the details of your essay, you must include an in-text citation between parentheses. This is often (but not always) placed at the end of a sentence, with the parentheses closed before the period. The most common way to indicate the source in your in-text citation is to use the author's last name and a page number. There are a couple of specific details, however, worth noting: First, if you choose to mention the author's name, clearly stated in your sentence, it is not necessary to include it inside the parentheses; you can simply use the page number in its place. Second, sometimes you might use more than one source by the same author; in that case, you will need to add the shortened title of the work (italicized if it is a book, or in quotation marks if it is an article) to make it clear which source by the author you are citing. In Zabdi Salazar's sample essay below, this example is illustrated by the author Melissa W. Wright, because Zabdi used two articles by this author.

It is critical to remember that the in-text citation information must match the same aspects of the same source in your works-cited list. Use a separate page for this information and title it "Works Cited." Examples below will demonstrate these details, and the section of this appendix titled "Further Reading and Resources" will provide you with free, critical Internet resources that will offer you various details not included here.

Books

SINGLE-AUTHOR BOOK

Works-Cited Format:

Author's Last Name, First Name. *Book Title*. Publisher, year.

Notice the use of commas and periods in the entry above. If the publisher of a book is a university press, the letters "U" and "P" are used as abbreviations. Only the publisher's name is necessary; the place of publication will be left out. Entries should not be numbered, but they will need to be in alphabetical order by the author's or authors' last name(s). If you include more than one source by the same author, alphabetize those works by title. If no author's name is available, list alphabetically by title of document.

Works-Cited List Examples:

Anzaldúa, Gloria E. *Borderlands / La Frontera: The New Mestiza*. Aunt
    Lute, 1987.
Aldama, Frederick Luis. *The Routledge Concise History of Latino/a Literature*. Routledge, 2013.

In-Text Citation Format:

(Author's Last Name page number)

Note: The parenthesis includes this information with no punctuation between the two items.

In-Text Citation Examples:
(Anzaldúa 8)
(Aldama 19)

If, for example, your works-cited list contains multiple works by Gloria E. Anzaldúa, then you would clarify which source you are citing by adding a shortened title; choose meaningful word(s) to shorten the title. A comma is used between the author's name and the shortened title, but not between the title and the page number.

(Anzaldúa, *Borderlands* 8)

BOOKS IN A LATER EDITION
Works-Cited Example:
Anzaldúa, Gloria E. *Borderlands/La Frontera: The New Mestiza*. 2nd ed., Aunt Lute, 1999.

In-Text Citation Example:
(Anzaldúa 8)

Note how, even for later editions, your in-text citations only need to include the author's last name (with shortened title if necessary to clarify) and the page number(s) you used.

Book Chapters
SINGLE CHAPTER FROM AN EDITED ANTHOLOGY/COLLECTION
If using a chapter from an edited anthology, you must include author's name and chapter title as well as the title of the anthology, the editor's name, the publisher, and the year of publication.

Works-Cited Examples:
Anzaldúa, Gloria. "To(o) Queer the Writer—Loca, escritora y chicana." *Living Chicana Theory*, edited by Carla Trujillo, Third Woman Press, 1997, pp. 263–76.

Gaspar de Alba, Alicia. "Thirty Years of Chicana/Latina Lesbian Literary Production." *The Routledge Companion to Latino/a Literature*,
edited by Suzanne Bost and Frances R. Aparicio, Routledge, 2015,
pp. 462–75.

In-Text Citation Examples:
You still need to include the author and page number in a parenthesis, ignoring the information about the larger anthology
in which the text is contained.

(Anzaldúa 268)
(Gaspar de Alba 463)

Periodicals
JOURNAL ARTICLES
Works-Cited Format:
Author's Last Name, First Name. "Title and Subtitle of Article." *Journal Name*, volume number, issue number, Date, page range of the
article.

If the article is electronic, the URL (uniform record locator, often
simply known as a web address) or DOI (digital object identifier)
follows the page numbers after a period.

Works-Cited List Examples:
Galarte, Francisco J. "On Trans* Chican@s: Amor, Justicia, y Dignidad."
Aztlán, vol. 39, no. 1, Spring 2014, pp. 229–36.
Sandoval, Chela. "U.S. Third World Feminism: The Theory and Method
of Oppositional Consciousness." *Genders*, vol. 10, Spring 1991,
pp. 1–23.

In-Text Citation Format:
(Galarte 230)
(Sandoval 22)

NEWSPAPER AND MAGAZINE ARTICLES
Note: If no author is listed, begin with the article title. Like journal articles, if a source is an online source, you must also include
its URL.

Works-Cited Format:
Author Last Name, First Name. "Title and Subtitle of Article." *Name of*
   Newspaper or Magazine, Date of Publication, page number(s), URL
   if an online publication.

Works-Cited List Example:
"El caso de los pachucos en manos de la embajada." *La Opinión*, 10
   June 1943, 1+.

In-Text Citation Example:
("El caso" 1)

Note: If the work in the works-cited list is filed under the title
because it has no named author, then the in-text citation will
also use that title, followed by the page number(s).

Interviews
PUBLISHED INTERVIEW
Works-Cited Format:
Last Name, First Name of Interviewee. "Title of Interview." Interview
   by First and Last Name of Interviewer. *Book Title*, Name of Editor,
   Publisher, Date, page range of interview.

Example:
Palacios, Monica. "Dos Lenguas Listas: An Interview with Monica Palacios, by Antonia Villaseñor." *Latinas on Stage*, edited by Alicia Arrizón and Lillian Manzor, Third Woman Press, 2000, pp. 234–47.

Note Example:
(Palacios 236)

FURTHER READING AND RESOURCES

The Modern Language Association is the leading authority on MLA-style citations. https://www.mla.org.

Owl Purdue: The Writing Lab at Purdue University has one of the most comprehensive reference guides for using MLA-style citations. https://owl.purdue.edu/owl/research_and_citation/mla_style/mla_formatting_and_style_guide/mla_formatting_and_style_guide.html.

Sample Student Literature / Cultural Studies Paper

Take note of the formatting this student, Zabdi J. Salazar, uses throughout her essay. A title page is optional in MLA style. It is more common to include the following information on the first page, at the top left corner: student name, class, and date. Zabdi begins with an epigraph, which offers an idea of her essay's stance and ties into her argument. The body of the paper is double-spaced, with no extra spaces between paragraphs. The longer quotations (those longer than four lines) are indented and double-spaced.

Zabdi J. Salazar

FYE 1600: First Year Experience: Inventing Mexico

Trinity University

November 25, 2015

The Devastating Effects of Neoliberalism on Democracy: The PAN's Twelve-Year Rule

> That is neoliberal democracy in a nutshell: trivial debate over minor issues by parties that basically pursue the same pro-business policies regardless of formal differences and campaign debate. Democracy is permissible as long as the control of business is off-limits to popular deliberation or change; i.e. so long as it isn't democracy.
>
> —Noam Chomsky, *Profit over People: Neoliberalism and Global Order*

During the social, political, and economic turmoil of the 1980s and 1990s in Mexico, grassroots organizations began to emerge and protest the imposed neoliberal policies of the authoritarian state government, the PRI (Institutional Revolutionary Party). These neoliberal programs and the state's authoritarian rule were fundamental in propagating extreme state violence. In effect, in the 2000 election, the direct impacts of the PRI's despotic rule on Mexican citizens led to its apparent loss of power for the first time in seventy years. That year, as opposition groups became stronger due to the PRI's loss of legitimacy, the PAN's (National Action Party) presidential candidate, Vicente Fox, won the presidency. Mexico and countries worldwide celebrated this significant peaceful and democratic transition of power. Unfortunately, the economic crisis from 2008 to 2010 revealed that there was no real change of power. Even though the new party's neoliberal economic agenda was now carried out by an assumed democratic and trusted leader, the voices of Mexican citizens remained oppressed. Although the PAN was given a second chance under Felipe Calderón, his declaration of the "War on Drugs" led to an unprecedented bloodbath. The party effectively avoided the country's real problems, which are rooted in a neoliberal economy. The PAN's short reign of twelve years of "democracy" sustained and promoted an authoritarian regime and extreme state violence, which continued to benefit only the elite classes through neoliberal policies.

To understand the false democratization of politics in the 2000 elections, the development of neoliberal policies and how they concentrate power must be addressed. Although after the overthrow of the dictator Porfirio Díaz in 1911 the government began instituting policies to reduce income gaps, such policies did not last. While the many causes of these shifts cannot be explored here, it is important to keep in mind that the neoliberal reforms of the 1980s followed years of broken promises (Harvey 39–40). It was the 1982 economic crisis, however, guided by neoliberal principles, that brought dramatic changes to Mexico's economy. These reforms subjugated the working class while the elite experienced profound economic growth (Muñoz Martínez; Treviso 34–35). The authoritarian government initiated programs to privatize national companies, use the lands of *campesinos* for agribusiness, establish maquiladoras, and sign free-trade agreements such as NAFTA.

Although President Carlos Salinas's administration created the PRONASOL solidarity program with the incentive to temporarily aid devastated sectors of the economy, in reality, the administration's efforts were focused on political campaigning to recover electoral support (Meyer 299). Thus, the government prioritized its assurance of maintaining political power and continuing its neoliberal policies. These attempts backfired on the PRI as citizens achieved electoral power. As Meyer summarizes:

[T]he sudden emergence of neoliberalism and its imposition of a radically new

economic model intensified economic, social, and political contradictions that

shaped two great opposition powers, the PAN and the PRD, provoked armed

uprising in Chiapas, and finally produced a citizens' "electoral revolt," which, after

several attempts, peacefully ended the seventy-one-year monopoly of the PRI in the

elections of July 2, 2000. (299)

Therefore, the 2000 elections represented Mexican citizens' denunciation of neoliberalism

and their future hopes for a reformative and responsive government under the PAN's

control. Unfortunately, a democratic transition of power cannot be equated with an

authentic democratic country.

Although Meyer optimistically stated that "the change of political parties was also a

regime change" (299), the PRI continued to monopolize control in Congress, thereby

limiting the power of the PAN to engage in meaningful reforms. Even though Vicente Fox

initiated some democratic changes such as open financial accounting in government, which

reduced corruption, these efforts were overturned during Calderón's power struggle with the

PRI in the 2008 economic crisis. This financial crisis also exposed the ill effects of an open

free market. As stated by Muñoz Martínez, "[T]he problem is that this economic model

continues to rely on the direct and indirect export of cheap labor through export processing

zones and immigration." The 2008 global crisis devastated Mexico's economy when its

domestic markets were weakened by economic programs that heavily interconnected it with

the U.S. economy and U.S. businesses. According to the United Nations Economic

Commission for Latin America and the Caribbean (ECLAC), Mexico was one of a few

Latin American nations in which poverty increased from 2006 to 2008 (Muñoz Martínez).

Salazar 4

Thus, the economic context was formed for the contradictory 2010 austerity budget, which failed to reduce state spending and increase frugal financial measures.

The alliance between the PRI and the PAN while generating the 2010 austerity budget highlighted the continuance of centralized rule and the limits of electoral liberalization. For example, the PRI allowed Calderón's proposal of a one percent increase in regressive taxation as long as more funds were channeled to state governments (most of which were controlled by the PRI) and transparency and accountability measures on state budgets were removed (Muñoz Martínez). Despite the economic crisis, the opposition parties also allowed such negotiations with the assurance that no cuts were made to the salaries of government officials, nor a limit placed on campaign spending (Muñoz Martínez). These fraudulent negotiations and the weakness of opposition parties, specifically the PRD, displayed how alliances with the PRI in Congress were essential for the passing of critical reforms, such as the state budget plan. Furthermore, although the IMF had advised different austerity measures such as evading regressive taxation and implementing a 2.5% deficit of the GDP, Mexico's authorities increased regressive taxes on the poor and working class to assuage the country's debt crisis (Muñoz Martínez). Thus, Mexico's rulers imposed undemocratic debts upon their citizenry.

Although Meyer had predicted that "incipient democracy had [given] Mexican neoliberalism a modern tone that it had been lacking" (274), in reality, the PAN's continuance of neoliberal economic policies proliferated state violence and exacerbated the devastating consequences of President Felipe Calderón's "War on Drugs." Calderón supported neoliberal trade programs such as NAFTA, ending tariffs for all agricultural goods in 2008 despite solid opposition by Mexican citizens. NAFTA facilitated the proliferation of drugs crossing the border since quicker access to U.S. markets allowed increased business. Furthermore, according to Laurell, the eradication of traditional agricultural crops by NAFTA contributed to the rise of the cultivation of marijuana and opium poppy (252). The implementation of the "War on Drugs" resulted from Calderón's need to portray legitimacy since many citizens deemed the close election race fraudulent. Such motivations had clearly been imprudent. The government did not expect a brutal battle against drug lords because they ignored the repercussions and connections between a neoliberal economy and the drug trade. Ultimately, Calderón also undermined democratic principles by engaging the military to fight drug cartels even though such action was forbidden by the constitution.

Structural violence is another consequence of neoliberal policies and economic agreements such as NAFTA, which has devastated the lives of many youths in border cities. Ciudad Juárez is now the murder capital of the world due to its impoverished communities and drug-related violence. Drug cartels are notorious for recruiting disenfranchised and jobless youth, *los ninis* (juveniles who do not work or study), by inciting them to kill in exchange for money. The rise of the maquiladoras has specifically displaced many young men since wages are low and corporate owners prefer women as a cheaper and docile labor source. Calderón's declaration of war against drug cartels also intensified the violence within the country as the killing of youth, "juvenicidio," has been normalized by the state (Wright, "Wars" 572). Unfortunately, the government's justification for its lack of accountability remains entrenched in the idea that such violence is between competing drug gangs (Wright, "Wars" 571). At the same time, the government often asserts that the horrendous murders of families and youth are because they had ties with drug cartels, to evade state responsibility.

Another terrible phenomenon in Ciudad Juárez has been increased killing of women since 1993. This "femicide" of female workers and students can be attributed, in part, to NAFTA, due to the rise of the maquiladora industries in bordering states. After 1993, the new job opportunities offered by the maquilas attracted women from rural and impoverished communities (Wright, "Wars" 571; Fussell 63–67). These factories exploited women by regarding them as disposable and cheap sources of labor. At the same time, Ciudad Juárez's drug cartels emerged in 1993, thus adding to the turmoil of an impoverished, violent, and crime-saturated city (Arriola 4).

Even more perplexing than the rise in violence, according to Wright, was the manner in which neoliberal politics temporarily succeeded in privatizing the murder of women by framing femicides as unimportant and a ubiquitous public matter ("Wars" 570). Corporate elites attempted to argue that such female victims "were looking to be murdered" (Wright, "Necropolitics" 714), implying that the murdered women were prostitutes and associates of cartels. After the consolidation of anti-femicide activists in 2003, the state's attorney general accused the activists of being opportunistic women who were "profiting with dead girls" (Wright, "Wars" 570). Thus, the government actively defeated any hope of ending structural violence. In sum, Wright describes the violent situation in Ciudad Juárez by stating:

> Some 10 years ago, the Mexican feminist activist, Esther Chávez . . . predicted that if the root causes of this violence were left in place, that the city would become "a horror," a place so torn by the relentless forces of capitalism, misogyny and despair that it would become unlivable. . . . The prescience of her words was revealed within

her lifetime. Shortly after the death of Chávez in December 2009, some bodies were dumped near her home, in what is now a regular occurrence across the city, in the poor and elite areas, on public and private property. ("Wars" 564)

Such lawlessness and lack of justice within border cities remain an epidemic. A state entrenched with corruption, impunity, and the lack of accountability is thereby intensified by neoliberal policies. As noted by Arriola, "[Y]ou can't separate the murders from the . . . indifference to the health and safety of the workers employed by the large and powerful NAFTA factories" (7).

Neoliberal democracy in Mexico has only proliferated the continuance of authoritarian power, the violence from the war on drugs, and the violation of human rights. Although political scientists and society worldwide hailed the 2000 elections as democratic, Mexico's neoliberal ideology and its undemocratic institutions have been a fundamental source of the government's authoritarian power. The failure of the PAN's regime to generate substantial reform was rooted in undemocratic institutions, which centralized power. Gridlock within Congress partly explained Fox's and Calderón's failure to address the violence and human rights violations that many Mexicans experienced because of neoliberalism. Although the election of Vicente Fox created a façade of democracy, and Felipe Calderón initially did the same for justice, the uncontrollable reign of a neoliberal economy centralized the rule and power of the government at the expense of working-class citizens.

Salazar 8

Works Cited

Arriola, Elvia R. "Justice Interrupted: The Ciudad Juárez Femicides and Global Social Responsibility."
      Voz de Esperanza, vol. 23, no. 2, 2010, pp. 3–7. *This Bridge Called Cyberspace*,
      thisbridgecalledcyberspace.net.

Fussell, Elizabeth. "Making Labor Flexible: The Recomposition of Tijuana's Maquiladora Female Labor
      Force." *Feminist Economics*, vol. 6, no. 3, 2000, pp. 59–79.

Harvey, Neil. "Rebellion in Chiapas: Rural Reforms and Popular Struggle." *Third World Quarterly*, vol.
      16, no. 1, 1995, pp. 39–73.

Laurell, Asa Cristina. "Three Decades of Neoliberalism in Mexico: The Destruction of Society."
      International Journal of Health Services, vol. 45, no. 2, April 2015, pp. 246–64. *Sage Journals*,
      https://doi.org/10.1177/0020731414568507.

Meyer, Lorenzo. "The Second Coming of Mexican Liberalism: A Comparative Perspective." *Cycles of
      Conflict, Centuries of Change: Crisis, Reform, and Revolution*, edited by Elisa Servin, Leticia
      Reina, and John Tutino, Duke UP, 2007, pp. 271–302.

Muñoz Martinez, Hepzibah. "Crisis, Populist Neoliberalism and the Limits to Democracy in Mexico."
      Europe Solidaire Sans Frontières, 15 December 2009, https://www.europe
      -solidaire.org/spip.php?article15918.

Treviso, Dolores. *Rural Protest and the Making of Democracy in Mexico, 1986–2000*. Pennsylvania State
      UP, 2011.

Wright, Melissa W. "Necropolitics, Narcopolitics, and Femicide: Gendered Violence on the Mexico-U.S.
      Border." *Signs*, vol. 36, no. 3, March 2011, pp. 707–31.

Wright, Melissa W. "The 2010 Antipode RGS-IBG Lecture: Wars of Interpretations." *Antipode*, vol. 44,
      no. 3, 2012, pp. 564–80. Wiley Online Library, https://doi.org/10.1111/j.1467-8330
      .2012.00991.x.

Online Archives and Resources

Calisphere, University of California

https://calisphere.org/

This is a collection of images from archives throughout California. The collection is very large. If you search for "Chicana," for example, you will find over one thousand images. So be sure to narrow your topic when using this collection. They do have some images by Chicanx and Latinx artists, as well as images of famous organizers such as Dolores Huerta, flyers and posters from political events, etc.

Catholic News Archive

https://thecatholicnewsarchive.org/

Over 30,000 issues of Catholic newspapers including the *Catholic Worker* and *La Esperanza*.

Chicana por mi Raza

https://chicanapormiraza.org/

In their own words, "Chicana por mi Raza Digital Memory Collective is a group of researchers, educators, students, archivists and technologists dedicated to preserving imperiled Chicanx and Latinx histories of the long Civil Rights Era. Started by Professor María Cotera and filmmaker Linda Garcia Merchant in 2009, CPMR has traveled to over one dozen states to collect hundreds of hours of oral histories with notable Chicanas, Latinas, and allies. The project has also scanned personal archives for preservation and access."

Farmworker Movement Documentation Project

https://libraries.ucsd.edu/farmworkermovement/archives/

Housed at the University of California, San Diego, the archive is a cornucopia of newsletters, interviews, images, and other primary documents of, by, and about people involved in the United Farm Workers union and movement. It contains a full run of *El Malcriado*.

La Onda Latina: The Mexican American Experience

http://www.laits.utexas.edu/onda_latina/

Organized and made available to the public by the University of Texas at Austin, the archive has images, interviews, speeches, and music recorded from the radio series *The Mexican American Experience* and *A esta hora conversamos*. The interviews are as diverse as "Interviews with Farm Workers in the Rio Grande Valley of Texas" and "Political Unrest in El Salvador."

Latinopia

https://latinopia.com/

A cultural resource page with art, history, literature, and much, much more. Contains some primary material including movement documents/mini-documentaries and interviews with activists.

Palante, NYU Libraries

http://dlib.nyu.edu/palante/

Palante was the newspaper of the Young Lords Party. It was published from 1970 to 1976. Housed at New York University, this is the most complete collection of the paper available online.

Seattle Civil Rights & Labor History Project, Chicana/o Movement in Washington

http://depts.washington.edu/civilr/mecha_intro.htm

Housed at the University of Washington, this site hosts documents, newspaper clippings, and oral histories from the Chicano Movement in the Pacific Northwest, including a video oral history of Yolanda Alaniz, co-author of *Viva la Raza: A History of Chicano Identity and Resistance*. It also has timelines, photos, and a slide show.

This Bridge Called Cyberspace

https://thisbridgecalledcyberspace.net/

This website is the host of over forty volumes of *Chicana/Latina Studies: The Journal of Mujeres Activas en Letras y Cambio Social* as well as other journals and newsletters such as *La Voz de Esperanza, Latin@ Literatures, Nakum,* and *Save Our Youth.* Here you will find academic articles, poetry, visual art, opinion pieces, and other sources.

Voices from the Gaps

https://conservancy.umn.edu/handle/11299/164018

Biographies and bibliographies about women writers of color, including Gloria Anzaldúa, Carmen Tafolla, and more. Excellent tertiary source, with some interviews that can function as primary sources. Most information is found under "artist pages."

NOTES

INTRODUCTION

1. Cherríe Moraga, "Giving Up the Ghost," in *Heroes and Saints and Other Plays* (Albuquerque: West End, 1994), 35.
2. Karen Mary Davalos, "Sin Vergüenza: Chicana Feminist Theorizing," *Feminist Studies* 34, nos. 1–2 (Spring/Summer 2008): 164–65.
3. Irene Isabel Blea, *Researching Chicano Communities: Social-Historical, Physical, Psychological, and Spiritual Space* (Westport, Conn.: Praeger, 1995), 27.
4. Blea, *Researching Chicano Communities*, 50–55.
5. Lawrence La Fountain-Stokes, "Queering Latina/o Literature," in *The Cambridge Companion to Latina/o American Literature*, ed. John Morán González (New York: Cambridge University Press, 2016), 186.
6. Virginia Sánchez Korrol, "The Origins and Evolution of Latino History," *OAH Magazine of History* 10, no. 2 (Winter 1996): 6.
7. Sánchez Korrol, "Origins and Evolution," 6; Nicole Trujillo-Pagán, "Recovering Latinos' Place in New Orleans," *Louisiana History* 55, no. 2 (Spring 2014): 177–97 (see p. 189 for her discussion of *El Misisipí*); Tom Reilly, "A Spanish-Language Voice of Dissent in Antebellum New Orleans," *Louisiana History* 23, no. 4 (Autumn 1982): 325–39.
8. These terms are utilized by Alicia Arrizón in *Latina Performance: Traversing the Stage* (Bloomington: Indiana University Press, 1999), 5. See also Sánchez Korrol, "Origins and Evolution," 5–12.
9. Rosaura Sánchez, Beatrice Pita, and Bárbara Reyes, *Nineteenth Century Californio Testimonial*, Crítica Monograph Series (San Diego: UCSD Ethnic Studies / Third World Studies, 1994); Rosaura

Sánchez, *Telling Identities: The Californio Testimonios* (Minneapolis: University of Minnesota Press, 1995); Lisbeth Haas, *Conquests and Historical Identities in California, 1769–1936* (Berkeley: University of California Press, 1995). In our historical oversimplification, our intent is not to negate the violent and devastating history of Spanish colonization imposed on the Indigenous populations in the territory that was renamed "New Spain" first and "Mexico" second. See Antonia I. Castañeda, "Sexual Violence in the Politics of Conquest: Amerindian Women and the Spanish Conquest of Alta California," in *Building with Our Hands: New Directions in Chicana Studies*, ed. Adela de la Torre and Beatriz M. Pesquera (Berkeley: University of California Press, 1993).

10. For more details on Puerto Rican history and identity, see Juan Flores, ed., *Between Borders* (Houston: Arte Público, 1993).

11. This civic status privilege for Puerto Ricans has been analyzed by Alberto Sandoval-Sánchez, especially in the face of the anti-immigrant and anti-undocumented bashing in the post–September 11 "terrorist hysteria." See Alberto Sandoval-Sánchez, "Imagining Puerto Rican Queer Citizenship: Frances Negrón-Muntaner's *Brincando el charco*: Portrait of a Puerto Rican," in *None of the Above: Puerto Ricans in the Global Era*, ed. Frances Negrón-Muntaner (New York: Palgrave Macmillan, 2007), 147–64.

12. Samoa and the U.S. Virgin Islands, although each with its own history of colonialism, also have a similar status as "U.S. territories."

13. Clara Rodríguez, Virginia Sánchez Korrol, and José Oscar Alers, "The Puerto Rican Struggle to Survive in the U.S.," in *Historical Perspectives on Puerto Rican Survival in the U.S.*, ed. Clara Rodríguez and Virginia Sánchez Korrol, 3rd ed. (Princeton: Markus Wiener Publishers, 1996), 1–10.

14. In 2003, Nilo Cruz, a gay Cuban American writer, became the first Latino playwright to receive the Pulitzer Prize in drama. His play *Anna in the Tropics* details the lives and struggles of Cuban tobacco and cigar workers in Florida during 1929. For more details on Cuban migration, see Nicolás Kanellos and Jorge A. Huerta, eds., *Nuevos Pasos: Chicano and Puerto Rican Drama* (Houston: Arte Público, 1989).

15. Arrizón, *Latina Performance*, 15. See also Iraida H. López, *Impossible Returns: Narratives of the Cuban Diaspora* (Gainesville: University Press of Florida, 2015); and Julio Capó Jr., "Queering Mariel: Mediating Cold War Foreign Policy and U.S. Citizenship

Among Cuba's Homosexual Exile Community, 1978–1994," *Journal of American Ethnic History* 29, no. 4 (2010): 78–106, https://doi.org/10.5406/jamerethnhist.29.4.0078.

16. Nora Hamilton and Norma Stoltz Chinchilla, *Seeking Community in a Global City: Guatemalans and Salvadorans in Los Angeles* (Philadelphia: Temple University Press, 2001), 27–32; Russell Crandall, *America's Dirty Wars: Irregular Warfare from 1776 to the War on Terror* (New York: Cambridge University Press, 2014), 239–44; Roberto García Ferreira, "La Revolución Guatemalteca y el legado del Presidente Árbenz," *Anuario de Estudios Centroamericanos* 38 (2012): 68–69, http://www.jstor.org/stable/43871192.

17. Crandall, *America's Dirty Wars*, 239–44; Douglas Farah, "Papers Show U.S. Role in Guatemalan Abuses: In Declassified Documents, Diplomats Describe Massacres, CIA Ties to Army," *International Journal of Health Services* 29, no. 4 (1999): 898. Quotation is from Farah.

18. Hamilton and Chinchilla, *Seeking Community*, 30–34.

19. Hamilton and Chinchilla, *Seeking Community*, 51, 135. Hamilton and Chinchilla note that in 1984 only 2.4 percent of Salvadoran and 0.4 percent of Guatemalans applying for asylum were granted status.

20. Ronald L. Mize, *Latina/o Studies* (Cambridge, UK: Polity, 2019), 23.

21. Michelle Téllez, "Doing Research at the Borderlands: Notes from a Chicana Feminist Ethnographer," *Chicana/Latina Studies* 4, no. 2 (Spring 2005): 49.

22. Sánchez Korrol, "Origins and Evolution," 6; David Gutiérrez, *Walls and Mirrors: Mexican Americans, Mexican Immigrants, and the Politics of Ethnicity* (Berkeley: University of California Press, 1995), 34–36, 95–100.

23. Christine Beagle García, "Siete Lenguas: The Rhetorical History of Dolores Huerta and the Rise of Chicana Rhetoric" (PhD dissertation, University of New Mexico, Albuquerque, 2015), 88.

24. William D. Carrigan and Clive Webb, *Forgotten Dead: Mob Violence Against Mexicans in the United States, 1848–1928* (New York: Oxford University Press, 2013), 117–19.

25. Yolanda Alaniz and Megan Cornish, *Viva la Raza: A History of Chicano Resistance* (Seattle: Red Letter Press, 2008), 116, 234.

26. José "Cha Cha" Jiménez, "The Young Lords, Puerto Rican Liberation, and the Black Freedom Struggle," *OAH Magazine of History* 26, no. 1 (2012): 61.

27. Johanna Fernández, "Denise Oliver and the Young Lords Party: Stretching the Political Boundaries of Struggle," in *Want to Start a Revolution? Radical Women in the Black Freedom Struggle*, ed. Dayo F. Gore, Jeanne Theoharris, and Woodard Komozi (New York: NYU Press, 2009), 271–93.
28. Fernández, "Denise Oliver," 282.
29. Mirta Vidal, *Chicanas Speak Out* (New York: Pathfinder Press, 1971), 6. Available at https://library.duke.edu/digitalcollections/wlmpc_wlmms01005/.
30. "Young Lords 13-Point Program and Platform," Latino Education Network Service, Palante.org, June 24, 2020, http://palante.org/YLPProg.html.
31. Full list available at http://palante.org/13%20Pt%20Program-1st.htm and in the appendices of this volume.
32. Richard Griswold del Castillo and Richard A. García, *César Chávez: A Triumph of the Spirit* (Norman: University of Oklahoma, 1995), 41–95; Alaniz and Cornish, *Viva la Raza*, 150–60.
33. Alaniz and Cornish, *Viva la Raza*, 191–92; Rodolfo Acuña, *Occupied America: A History of Chicanos*, 7th ed. (Boston: Pearson, 2007), 308.
34. "El Plan Espiritual de Aztlán," Latinopia.com, accessed July 17, 2020, http://latinopia.com/latino-history/plan-de-aztlan/.
35. "El Plan de Santa Bárbara," Latinopia.com, accessed July 17, 2020, http://latinopia.com/latino-history/latinopia-document-el-plan-de-santa-barbara/.
36. Judith K. Brodsky and Ferris Olin, *Junctures in Women's Leadership: The Arts* (New Brunswick: Rutgers University Press, 2018), 82–92, ProQuest Ebook Central.
37. Teatro Chicana's collection of plays was published by the University of Texas Press's Chicana Matters series in 2008. In 1974, Moreno's group wrote and performed the play *Chicana*, which traced Chicanas' historical ancestors such as Sor Juana Inés de la Cruz and the Adelitas. See Yvonne Yarbro-Bejarano, "Chicanas' Experience in Collective Theater," *Women and Perfomance* 2, no. 2 (1985): 45–48; and Yolanda Broyles-González, *El Teatro Campesino: Theater in the Chicano Movement* (Austin: University of Texas Press, 1994), for a more detailed discussion of women's participation in theater in the 1960s and 1970s.
38. "History," National Association for Chicana and Chicano Studies, accessed May 20, 2022, https://www.naccs.org/naccs/History.asp.

39. Hamilton and Chinchilla, *Seeking Community*, 66; Ester Hernández, "Remembering Through Cultural Interventions: Mapping Central Americans in L.A. Public Spaces," in *U.S. Central Americans: Reconstructing Memories, Struggles, and Communities of Resistance*, ed. Karina O. Alvarado, Alicia Ivonne Estrada, and Ester E. Hernández (Tucson: University of Arizona Press, 2017), 154–55; Norma Stoltz Chinchilla, Nora Hamilton, and James Loucky, "The Sanctuary Movement and Central American Activism in Los Angeles," *Latina American Perspectives* 36, no. 6 (2009): 108.

40. Hamilton and Chinchilla, *Seeking Community*, 74–87; Norma Chinchilla and Nora Hamilton, "Changing Networks and Alliances in a Transnational Context: Salvadoran and Guatemalan Immigrants in Southern California," *Social Justice* 26, no. 3 (1999): 8.

41. Hamilton and Chinchilla, *Seeking Community*, 120–21, 128–29.

42. "Wayne State University's Center for Chicano-Boricua Studies Program Honored Nationally for Increasing Degree Completion Among Latinos," *La Prensa*, November 11, 2011, 4; Refugio I. Rochin and Adaljisa Sosa-Riddell, "Chicano Studies in a Pluralistic Society: Contributing to Multiculturalism," *Bilingual Review* 17, no. 2 (May–August 1992): 11. In the last decade, the University of California Santa Barbara and UCLA both expanded their departments to offer PhDs in Chicana/o studies; the University of Wyoming expanded its course offerings and established a Chicano studies program in its College of Arts and Sciences, which later expanded to Latinx studies. See "The Department of Chicana/o Studies," UC Santa Barbara, Chicano Studies, accessed June 26, 2023, https://www.chicst.ucsb.edu/about; "History & Background of the UCLA César E. Chávez Department of Chicana/o and Central American Studies," UCLA César E. Chávez Department of Chicana/o and Central American Studies, accessed June 26, 2023, https://chavez.ucla.edu/about/history/; and Ed A. Muñoz, Angela M. Jaime, Deborah L. McGriff, and Adrian H. Molina, "Assessment of Student Learning: Estudios Chicana/o Cultivating Critical Cultural Thinking," *Teaching Sociology* 40, no. 1 (2012): 34–49, http://www.jstor.org/stable/41503321.

43. Hamilton and Chinchilla, *Seeking Community*, 198–99.

44. Katherine Schaeffer, "In a Rising Number of U.S. Counties, Hispanic and Black Americans Are the Majority," *FACTANK: News in*

Numbers, Pew Research Center, November 20, 2019, https://www
.pewresearch.org/fact-tank/2019/11/20/in-a-rising-number-of-u
-s-counties-hispanic-and-black-americans-are-the-majority/.
45. "Hispanic Heritage Month 2019," United States Census Bureau,
August 20, 2019, https://www.census.gov/newsroom/facts-for
-features/2019/hispanic-heritage-month.html.
46. William H. Frey, "The US Will Become 'Minority White' in 2045,
Census Projects: Youthful Minorities Are the Engine of Future Growth," Brookings Institute, March 14, 2018, https://www
.brookings.edu/blog/the-avenue/2018/03/14/the-us-will-become
-minority-white-in-2045-census-projects/.

CHAPTER 1

1. Gervasio Luis García, "I Am the Other: Puerto Rico in the Eyes
of North Americans, 1898," *Journal of American History* 87, no. 1
(2000): 49–51, https://doi.org/10.2307/2567915. García notes
how, in their debates regarding whether to call Puerto Rico by the
name its people chose for it or to call it "Porto Rico," which would
be easier for Euro-Americans to pronounce, American politicians
and businessmen did not consult Puerto Ricans.
2. Patricia Seed, "Social Dimensions of Race: Mexico City, 1753,"
Hispanic American Historical Review 62, no. 4 (1982): 569–606,
https://doi.org/10.2307/2514568. See also Stafford Poole, "Church
Law on the Ordination of Indians and Castas in New Spain," *Hispanic American Historical Review* 61, no. 4 (1981): 637–50, https://
doi.org/10.2307/2514607; Douglas Cope, *The Limits of Racial
Domination: Plebeian Society in Colonial Mexico City, 1660–1720*
(Madison: University of Wisconsin Press, 1994), 19–41.
3. For a more detailed discussion of the colonial casta system and
its relationship to social class and ethnicity (especially as related
to Mexico), see Cope, *Limits of Racial Domination*; and Adrian
Bustamante, "'The Matter Was Never Resolved': The 'Casta' System in Colonial New Mexico, 1693–1823," *New Mexico Historical
Review* 66, no. 2 (1991): 143.
4. Seed, "Social Dimensions," 591–602.
5. Laura Quiros and Beverly Araujo Dawson, "The Color Paradigm:
The Impact of Colorism on the Racial Identity and Identification
of Latinas," *Journal of Human Behavior in the Social Environment*
23, no. 3 (2013): 287–97, https://doi.org/10.1080/10911359.2012
.740342.

6. Elizabeth Martínez, *De Colores Means All of Us: Latina Views for a Multi-colored Century* (Cambridge, Mass.: South End Press, 1988), 2–3.

7. E. Martínez, *De Colores*, 3.

8. Paul Ortiz, *An African American and Latinx History of the United States* (Boston: Beacon Press, 2018), 42–48; David E. Narrett, "A Choice of Destiny: Immigration Policy, Slavery, and the Annexation of Texas," *Southwestern Historical Quarterly* 100, no. 3 (1997): 276–80, http://www.jstor.org/stable/30239099.

9. Vicki L. Ruiz, "Nuestra América: Latino History as United States History," *Journal of American History* 93, no. 3 (2006): 658–60, https://doi.org/10.2307/4486408.

10. Gloria Anzaldúa, *Borderlands / La Frontera: The New Mestiza* (San Francisco: Aunt Lute, 1987), 3.

11. Laura Pulido and Manuel Pastor, "Where in the World Is Juan—and What Color Is He? The Geography of Latina/o Racial Identity in Southern California," *American Quarterly* 65, no. 2 (2013): 311, http://www.jstor.org/stable/43823097.

12. Suzanne Oboler, *Ethnic Labels, Latino Lives: Identity and the Politics of (Re)presentation in the United States* (Minneapolis: University of Minnesota Press, 1995), 36–38; Ronald L. Mize, *Latina/o Studies* (Cambridge, UK: Polity, 2019), 22; G. García, "I Am the Other," 46.

13. G. García, "I Am the Other," 43–44.

14. Mize, *Latina/o Studies*, 21.

15. L Heidenreich, *Nepantla Squared: Transgender Mestiz@ Histories in Times of Global Shift* (Lincoln: University of Nebraska Press, 2020), 94; Rafael Hernández, "Alliances and Dis-alliances Between the United States and Latin America and the Caribbean," *Latin American Perspectives* 178, no. 4 (July 2011): 131–36.

16. Rámon Gutiérrez, "What's in a Name?," in *The New Latino Studies Reader: A Twenty-First-Century Perspective*, ed. Ramón Gutiérrez and Tomás Almaguer (Oakland: University of California Press, 2016), 19–52.

17. Manuel Pastor, "Latinos and the New American Majority," *Dissent* 63, no. 3 (2016): 56, https://doi.org/10.1353/dss.2016.0049. For details on how the U.S. government mobilizes this term, see Mize, *Latina/o Studies*, 2–4.

18. Pastor, "New American Majority," 56. See Oboler, *Ethnic Labels*, 81, for a discussion of Richard Nixon's 1969 proclamation.

19. Oboler, *Ethnic Labels*, 10.
20. José Limón, "The Folk Performance of 'Chicano' and the Cultural Limits of Political Ideology" (Sociolinguist Working Paper 62, Southwest Educational Development Laboratory, Austin, Tex., 1979).
21. Arnoldo De León and Richard Griswold del Castillo, *North to Aztlán: A History of Mexican Americans in the United States* (Malden: Wiley and Blackwell, 2006), 158–59; Oboler, *Ethnic Labels*, 58–69.
22. Oboler, *Ethnic Labels*, 65.
23. José Ángel Gutiérrez, "The Chicano Movement: Paths to Power," *Social Studies* 102, no. 1 (2010): 25–32, https://doi.org/10.1080/00377996.2011.533043; Mize, *Latina/o Studies*, 32.
24. Juan Gómez Quiñones, *Chicano Politics: Reality and Promise, 1940–1990* (Albuquerque: University of New Mexico Press, 1992), 128–29.
25. Johanna Fernández, *The Young Lords: A Radical History* (Chapel Hill: University of North Carolina Press, 2020), 344–59, 375; Oboler, *Ethnic Labels*, 57.
26. Elizabeth Coonrod Martínez and Gabriela Baeza Ventura, "A History of Latino-Focused Journals and Collaborative Research," *Diálogo* 20, no. 2 (2017): 1–6, https://doi.org/10.1353/dlg.2017.0027; Rose Miyatsu, "Celebrating Hispanic Heritage with *Revista Chicano-Riqueña*," Washington University in St. Louis University Libraries, September 18, 2018, accessed February 6, 2022, https://library.wustl.edu/news/celebrating-hispanic-heritage-with-revista-chicano-riquena/.
27. Felix M. Padilla, *Latino Ethnic Consciousness: The Case of Mexican Americans and Puerto Ricans in Chicago* (Notre Dame, Ind.: University of Notre Dame Press, 1985), 13–14.
28. A simple search online about Latinx actors returns Spaniards like Penélope Cruz and Javier Bardem, for example. The use of this term in popular culture erases, once again, the major differences that Oboler and others have discussed regarding race/ethnicity, histories, and other privileges.
29. Francisco J. Galarte, "Transgender Chican@ Poetics: Contesting, Interrogating and Transforming Chicana/o Studies," *Chicana/Latina Studies* 13, no. 2 (Spring 2014): 135n2.
30. Aída Hurtado, *Intersectional Chicana Feminisms* (Tucson: University of Arizona Press, 2020), 11.

31. The racist and nativist sentiments against the Chinese in the late 1880s and the Japanese during World War II forced members of both ethnic groups to migrate permanently to Mexico, especially to states like Baja California, Sonora, Sinaloa, and Chihuahua.

32. Jennie Luna and Gabriel S. Estrada, "Trans*lating the Gender-queer -*X* Through Caxcan, Nahua, and Xicanx Indígena Knowledge," in *Decolonizing Latinx Masculinities*, ed. Arturo J. Aldama and Frederick Luis Aldama (Tucson: University of Arizona Press, 2020), 251–68. For an earlier use of the *X* associated with the term *Chicana*, see also Ana Castillo, who in 1994 published her book *Massacre of the Dreamers: Essays on Xicanisma* (Albuquerque: University of New Mexico Press, 1994).

33. L Heidenreich with Antonia I. Castañeda, eds., *Three Decades of Engendering History: Selected Works of Antonia I. Castañeda* (Denton: University of North Texas Press, 2014), 283.

34. Amelia Montes, "The Lesbian Caucus Has a New Name: The Lesbian, Bisexual Mujeres, Trans Caucus," *Noticias de NACCS* 35, no. 1 (Summer 2006).

35. Raúl Coronado, "Joto Caucus," *Noticias de NACCS* 28, no. 2 (June 2001): 7; L Heidenreich, "Queer Turns: NACCS XLV and the Call to 'Queer the World in a Lot of Different Ways,'" in *NACCS Annual Conference Proceedings* 3 (2018): 4, https://scholarworks.sjsu.edu/cgi/viewcontent.cgi?article=1194&context=naccs.

36. Gloria E. Anzaldúa, "To(o) Queer the Writer—Loca, escritora y chicana," in *The Gloria Anzaldúa Reader*, ed. AnaLouise Keating (Durham: Duke University Press, 2009), 164.

37. Anita Tijerina Revilla, "The Association for Jotería Arts, Activism, and Scholarship," *Aztlán* 39, no. 1 (Spring 2014): 253–59. MALCS, traditionally a Chicana/Latina/Indigenous women's organization, also changed its bylaws to be more inclusive as "a professional organization for self-identified Chicana, Latina, Native American / Indígena mujeres and gender non-conforming academics, students, and activists."

38. Michael Hames-García, "Jotería Studies, or the Political Is Personal," *Aztlán* 39, no. 1 (Spring 2014): 137.

39. Hames-García, "Jotería Studies," 137.

40. "Vision," Association for Jotería Arts, Activism, and Scholarship, accessed July 14, 2022, https://www.ajaas.com/mandv. See also Tijerina Revilla, "Association," 258.

41. Anzaldúa, "To(o) Queer the Writer," 163.

42. Alicia Gaspar de Alba, "Making Tortillas," in *Three Times a Woman: Chicana Poetry*, ed. Alicia Gaspar de Alba, María Herrera-Sobek, and Demetria Martínez (Tempe: Bilingual Review, 1989), 44–45.

43. Lourdes Torres, introduction to *Tortilleras: Hispanic and U.S. Latina Lesbian Expression*, ed. Lourdes Torres and Inmaculada Pertusa (Philadelphia: Temple University Press, 2003), 6.

44. Daniel Enrique Pérez, "Toward a Mariposa Consciousness: Reimagining Queer Chicano and Latino Identities," *Aztlán* 39, no. 2 (Fall 2014): 95–127. The work of Alma López, Julio Salgado, and Tino Rodríguez, as well as various queer Latina/o/x anthologies and single-author books released since the beginning of this century, helped establish new versions of these fields of study and the use of the mariposa as an expression of gay and undocuqueer (undocumented and queer) pride.

45. E. Martínez, *De Colores*, 3.

CHAPTER 2

Dr. L Heidenreich wrote this chapter, given their expertise and publications in these fields of study. They utilized the *Chicago Manual of Style* for their references so that they serve as examples for students who need to research and write in history.

1. Gloria Anzaldúa, *Borderlands / La Frontera: The New Mestiza* (San Francisco: Aunt Lute, 1987), 3.

2. Emma Pérez, *The Decolonial Imaginary: Writing Chicanas into History* (Bloomington: Indiana University Press, 1999), 6.

3. Rodolfo Acuña, *Sometimes There Is No Other Side: Chicanos and the Myth of Equality* (Notre Dame, Ind.: University of Notre Dame Press, 1998), 109–14.

4. George Isidore Sánchez, *Forgotten People* (Albuquerque: University of New Mexico Press, 1940); Jovita González, *The Woman Who Lost Her Soul*, ed. Sergio Reyna (Houston: Arte Público, 2001); Ernesto Galarza, *Merchants of Labor: The Mexican Bracero Story; An Account of the Managed Migration of Mexican Farm Workers in California, 1942–1960* (Charlotte: McNally and Loftin, 1964); Américo Paredes, *"With His Pistol in His Hand": A Border Ballad and Its Hero* (Austin: University of Texas Press, 1958). For historiographies addressing this foundational generation, see Deena J. González, "Gender on the Borderlands: Re-textualizing the Classics," *Frontiers* 24, no. 2/3 (2003): 15–29; and David G. Gutiérrez, "Significant to Whom? Mexican Americans and the

History of the American West," *Western Historical Quarterly* 24, no. 4 (1993): 519–39.

5. Acuña, *Sometimes There Is No Other Side*, 109–14.

6. Susanne Jonas, "In Memoriam: Frank Bonilla, Renaissance Man (1925–2010)," *Latin American Perspectives* 38, no. 3 (May 2011): 209–11; Ronald L. Mize, *Latina/o Studies* (Cambridge, UK: Polity, 2019), 39–40.

7. Clara E. Rodriguez, "Puerto Rican Studies," *American Quarterly* 42, no. 3 (September 1990): 437.

8. Lorena Oropeza and Dionne Espinoza, eds., *Enriqueta Vasquez and the Chicano Movement: Writings from "El Grito del Norte"* (Houston: Arte Público, 2006). See esp. "16 de septiembre," 43–46.

9. Gabriela González, *Redeeming La Raza: Transborder Modernity, Race, Respectability, and Rights* (New York: Oxford University Press, 2018), 25; Elizabeth Garner Masarik, "Por la Raza, para la Raza: Jovita Idar and Progressive-Era Mexicana Maternalism Along the Texas-Mexico Border," *Southwestern Historical Quarterly* 122, no. 3 (2019): 278–99. It was in 1914 that Idar famously stood up to the Texas Rangers, who threatened to destroy the press. They did return later and succeeded in destroying it. Idar went on to work in education and to write for other newspapers.

10. Ivette Romero-Cesareo, "Whose Legacy? Voicing Women's Rights from the 1870s to the 1930s," *Callaloo* 17, no. 3 (Summer 1994): 779–80.

11. Magali Roy-Fequiere, "Contested Territory: Puerto Rican Women, Creole Identity, and Intellectual Life in the Early Twentieth Century," *Callaloo* 17, no. 3 (Summer 1994): 928.

12. In fact, this was a theme throughout Chicanx studies. Blea, for example, noted that we, as Chicanx scholars, must remind ourselves of "the self-evident but often forgotten truth that the U.S. is only one of many Latino countries in the Americas." Irene Isabel Blea, *Researching Chicano Communities: Social-Historical, Physical, Psychological, and Spiritual Space* (Westport: Praeger, 1995), 115. See also Maribel Ortiz Márquez, "Beginnings: Puerto Rican Studies Revisited," *Centro Journal* 21, no. 2 (2009): 183–86.

13. Kyle Steenland, "The Coup in Chile," *Latin American Perspectives* 1, no. 2 (Summer 1974): 22–29. The CIA and U.S. involvement is too extensive to document here. Steenland highlights that many officers at the U.S. embassy were CIA agents, and that the CIA had sent $400,000 to fund anti-Allende media campaigns (approved

by the National Security Council), had infiltrated "almost all political parties," and had played a "leading role in the assassination
of Allende's naval aide."

14. James Maffie, *Aztec Philosophy: Understanding a World in Motion*
    (Boulder: University of Colorado Press, 2014), 2–21.
15. Gloria Anzaldúa in Karin Rosa Ikas, *Chicana Ways: Conversations
    with Ten Chicana Writers* (Reno: University of Nevada, 2002), 13–
    14; Gloria E. Anzaldúa, "Let Us Be the Healing of the Wound: The
    Coyolxauhqui Imperative—La Sombra y el Sueño," in *One Wound
    for Another / Una Herida por Otra: Testimonios de Latin@s in the
    U.S. Through Cyberspace*, ed. Claire Joysmith and Clara Lomas
    (Mexico: Universidad Nacional Autónoma de México, 2005), 99.
    See also Emma Pérez, "Gloria Anzaldúa: La Gran Nueva Mestiza
    Theorist, Writer, Activist-Scholar," *NWSA Journal* 17, no. 2 (Sum-
    mer 2005).
16. Alma M. García, introduction to *Chicana Feminist Thought: The
    Basic Historical Writings*, ed. Alma M. García (New York: Rout-
    ledge, 1997), 8.
17. Martha Cotera, "Our Feminist Heritage," in *The Chicana Feminist*
    (Austin: Information Systems Development, 1977), 1–7.
18. Martha Cotera, "Chingona Chones y Nuevas Generaciones: A
    Reflection on *Diosa y Hembra*," *Chicana/Latina Studies* 19, no. 2
    (Spring 2020): 39.
19. Adaljiza Sosa Riddell, "Chicanas and el Movimiento," *Aztlán* 5,
    no. 1 (Spring 1974): 155–65.
20. María Linda Apodaca, "The Chicana Woman: An Historical Mate-
    rialist Perspective," *Latin American Perspectives* 4, no. 1/2 (Spring
    1977): 70–89, quotation at 72.
21. Rodolfo Acuña, *Occupied America: The Chicano's Struggle Toward
    Liberation* (San Francisco: Harper and Row, 1972), 2.
22. Acuña, *Occupied America*, 9–10.
23. Mario Trinidad García, review of *Occupied America: The Chica-
    no's Struggle Toward Liberation* by Rodolfo Acuña and *The Chi-
    canos: A History of Mexican Americans* by Matt S. Meier and Fe-
    liciano Rivera, *Pacific Historical Review* 43, no. 1 (1974): 123–25;
    Victor Dahl, review of *Occupied America: The Chicano's Struggle
    Toward Liberation* by Rodolfo Acuña, *Western Historical Quar-
    terly* 4, no. 3 (1973): 340.
24. Albert Camarillo, *Chicanos in a Changing Society: From Mexican
    Pueblos to American Barrios in Santa Barbara and Southern Cal-*

ifornia, 1848–1930 (Cambridge, Mass.: Harvard University Press, 1979); Ricardo Romo, *East Los Angeles: History of a Barrio* (Austin: University of Texas Press, 1983). See also Matt A. Meier and Feliciano Rivera, *The Chicanos: A History of Mexican Americans* (New York: Hill and Wang, 1972); Richard Griswold del Castillo, *La Familia: Chicano Families in the Urban Southwest, 1848 to the Present* (Notre Dame, Ind.: University of Notre Dame Press, 1984); Richard Griswold del Castillo, *The Los Angeles Barrio, 1850–1890: A Social History* (Berkeley: University of California Press, 1979); Arnoldo De León, *They Called Them Greasers: Anglo Attitudes Toward Mexicans in Texas, 1821–1900* (Austin: University of Texas Press, 1983); Gilberto Miguel Hinojosa, *A Borderlands Town in Transition: Laredo, 1755–1870* (College Station: Texas A&M University Press, 1983); and Mario T. García, *Desert Immigrants: The Mexicans of El Paso, 1880–1920* (New Haven: Yale University Press, 1981).

25. E. Pérez, *Decolonial Imaginary*, 21–22.

26. Albert Camarillo, Ricardo Romo, Richard Griswold del Castillo, and Pedro Castillo were the first generation of Chicano historians trained in U.S. history. The earlier generation of Chicana historians—Ana Macías, Luisa Año Nuevo Kerr, Raquel Rubio-Goldsmith, and Shirlene Soto—were, like their male counterparts, historians of Mexico and Latin America.

27. Vicki Ruiz, *Cannery Women, Cannery Lives: Mexican Women, Unionization, and the California Food Processing Industry, 1930–1950* (Albuquerque: University of New Mexico Press, 1987).

28. Adelaida R. Del Castillo, "Malintzin Tenépal: A Preliminary Look into a New Perspective," in *Essays on La Mujer*, ed. Rosaura Sánchez and Rosa Martínez Cruz (1973; repr., Los Angeles: Chicano Studies Center Publication, 1977), 125.

29. A. Del Castillo, "Malintzin Tenépal"; Norma Alarcón, "Chicana's Feminist Literature: A Re-vision Through Malintzin / or Malintzin: Putting Flesh Back on the Object," in *This Bridge Called My Back: Writings by Radical Women of Color*, ed. Cherríe Moraga and Gloria Anzaldúa (New York: Kitchen Table, 1983); Shirlene Soto, "Tres Modelos Culturales: La Virgen de Guadalupe, la Malinche y la Llorona," *Fem* 10 (1986): 13–16. See also Cordelia Candelaria, "La Malinche, Feminist Prototype," *Frontiers* 5, no. 2 (1980): 1–6.

30. Catrióna Rueda Esquibel, *With Her Machete in Her Hand: Reading Chicana Lesbians* (Austin: University of Texas Press, 2006), 25–26.

31. Anzaldúa, *Borderlands*, 29–31.

32. Deena J. González, "Gender on the Borderlands: Re-textualizing the Classics," *Frontiers* 24, nos. 2–3 (2003): 18.

33. Karina O. Alvarado, Alicia I. Estrada, and Ester E. Hernández, eds., *U.S. Central Americans: Reconstructing Memories, Struggles, and Communities of Resistance* (Tucson: University of Arizona Press, 2017).

34. Teresita Levy, *Puerto Ricans in the Empire: Tobacco Growers and U.S. Colonialism* (New York: Rutgers University Press, 2014); Victoria González-Rivera, *Before the Revolution: Women's Rights and Right-Wing Politics in Nicaragua, 1821–1979* (University Park: Penn State University Press, 2011); Yvette J. Saavedra, *Pasadena Before the Roses: Race, Identity, and Land Use in Southern California, 1771–1890* (Tucson: University of Arizona Press, 2018); Dionne Espinoza, María Eugenia Cotera, and Maylei Blackwell, eds., *Chicana Movidas: New Narratives of Activism and Feminism in the Movement Era* (Austin: University of Texas Press, 2018). At the time of this writing Levy was working on her third book, *500 Years of Nicaraguan LGBT History*.

35. Espinoza, Cotera, and Blackwell, *Chicana Movidas*, 11.

36. D. González, "Gender on the Borderlands," 16.

37. E. Pérez, *Decolonial Imaginary*, 27.

38. Blea, *Researching Chicano Communities*, 52–55.

39. Neil Gaiman quoted on Quote Investigator, https://quoteinvestigator.com/2016/04/23/library/.

40. E. Pérez, *Decolonial Imaginary*, xv–xvii.

41. Karen Mary Davalos, "Sin Vergüenza: Chicana Feminist Theorizing," *Feminist Studies* 34, nos. 1–2 (Spring/Summer 2008): 166.

42. Wayne C. Booth, Gregory C. Colomb, and Joseph M. Williams, *The Craft of Research*, 3rd ed. (Chicago: University of Chicago Press, 2008), 35–50.

43. Blea, *Researching Chicano Communities*, 98.

44. *Palante*, New York University Libraries, http://dlib.nyu.edu/palante/.

45. National Security Archive, https://nsarchive.gwu.edu/digital-national-security-archive.

CHAPTER 3

Dr. Rita E. Urquijo-Ruiz wrote this chapter, given her expertise and publications in these fields of study. She utilized the Modern

Language Association (MLA) manual of style for her references
so that they serve as examples for students who need to research
and write in these academic fields.

1. The full name of this international program is Recovering the
U.S. Hispanic Literary Heritage, launched by Arte Público Press
in Houston: https://artepublicopress.com/recovery-program/.

2. For an introduction to the term "nepantla," see Anzaldúa and Keating. See also Heidenreich.

3. For Latina playwrights of Cuban, Puerto Rican, and Dominican
descent, see the works of María Irene Fornés, Migdalia Cruz, Sandra María Esteves, and Caridad Svich. For performance artists,
see the works of Monica Palacios, Carmelita Tropicana, Marga
Gómez, and Adelina Anthony.

4. Chicana feminists and visionaries Alarcón and Castillo (contributors to *This Bridge*) collaborated with Moraga to publish a Spanish
translation of this manuscript, co-edited by Moraga and Castillo
and titled *Esta puente, mi espalda: Voces de mujeres tercermundistas en los Estados Unidos.* In this title, the word for "bridge," which
is usually a masculine noun in Spanish, is feminized by the de-
monstrative pronoun "esta," establishing the editors' and contributors' Third World feminism beginning with the first word the
reader captures on the book cover.

5. Following Anzaldúa's death from diabetes complications in May
2004, the Society for the Study of Gloria E. Anzaldúa (SSGA) was
established by lesbian writer, poet, and literary critic Norma Elia
Cantú and Chicana feminist scholar Sonia Saldívar-Hull along
with authors/scholars including Larissa Mercado-Lopez, Patricia
Trujillo, and Rita E. Urquijo-Ruiz. SSGA is located in San Antonio,
Texas, and its mission is to continue Anzaldúa's legacy and teach-
ings through an international conference titled "El Mundo Zurdo"
that happens primarily in San Antonio every eighteen months.
Aunt Lute has published selected works from each conference
in volumes 1–8 of *El Mundo Zurdo*, edited by various new and
established queer and feminist scholars. To date, *Borderlands* is
the best-selling title for the independent press Aunt Lute Books
located in San Francisco, California. The book has been translated into peninsular and Mexican Spanish, as well as French and
Italian. In 2012 the twenty-fifth-anniversary/fourth edition was
published, and in 2021 the critical edition by Ricardo F. Vivancos-
Pérez and Norma E. Cantú was also published by Aunt Lute Books.

6. Tatiana de la tierra preferred not to capitalize her name.

7. There are other terms used by Rebolledo that serve a similar purpose by alluding to rebel women: "atravesadas, escandalosas, trouble-makers, malcriadas, and wicked women." For more specific details about the minor variations on each term, see her chapter entitled "Mujeres Andariegas: Good Girls and Bad" (Rebolledo 183–206).

8. Anzaldúa encourages women of color to not fear being called a "sell-out" when fighting for self-empowerment. She states: "So mamá, Raza, how wonderful, *no tener que rendir cuentas a nadie.* I feel perfectly free to rebel and to rail against my culture. I fear no betrayal on my part. . . . To separate from my culture (as from my family) I had to feel competent enough on the outside and secure enough inside to live life on my own. . . . And if going home is denied me then I will have to stand and claim my space, making a new culture—*una cultura mestiza*—with my own lumber, my own bricks and mortar and my own feminist architecture" (Anzaldúa, *Borderlands* 21–22).

9. An earlier version of the essay "Let Us Be the Healing of the Wound: The Coyolxauhqui Imperative—La Sombra y el Sueño" was first published in Claire Joysmith and Clara Lomas's *One Wound for Another / Una Herida por Otra: Testimonios de Latin@s in the U.S. Through Cyberspace* (Universidad Nacional Autónoma de México, 2005).

10. Scholar.google.com is a better search engine to find "scholarly" work, rather than using a general Google search.

11. Thanks to the generous work of L. Justine Hernández, ThisBridge CalledCyberspace.net continues to offer, free of charge, over forty volumes of this journal, which can be accessed at https://thisbridgecalledcyberspace.net/index.php?pub_id=1.

12. An excellent source that details the steps of "close reading" of a text is the Harvard College Writing Center: https://writingcenter .fas.harvard.edu/pages/how-do-close-reading.

13. The library at California State University, Northridge, offers a great resource and plenty of examples of annotated bibliographies: https://libguides.csun.edu/research-strategies/annotated -bibliography.

CHAPTER 4

Dr. L Heidenreich wrote this chapter, given their expertise and publications in these fields of study. They utilized the *Chicago*

Manual of Style for their references, which is the preferred style for oral histories. Keep in mind that many fields use interviews, pláticas, and testimonios as sources. Some of these other fields may prefer MLA or APA citations.

1. Raquel Rubio-Goldsmith, "Oral History: Considerations and Problems for Its Use in the History of Mexicanas in the United States," in *Between Borders: Essays on Mexicana/Chicana History*, ed. Adelaida R. Del Castillo (Encino, Calif.: Floricanto Press, 1990), 162.

2. Lorena V. Márquez, "Recovering Chicana/o Movement History Through Testimonios," in *Community-Based Participatory Research: Testimonios from Chicana/o Studies*, ed. Natalia Deeb-Sossa and Louie F. Rodríguez (Tucson: University of Arizona Press, 2019), 94.

3. Vicki L. Ruiz, *Cannery Women, Cannery Lives: Mexican Women, Unionization, and the California Food Processing Industry, 1930–1950* (Albuquerque: University of New Mexico Press, 1987).

4. L. Márquez, "Recovering Chicana/o Movement History," 103; Natalia Deeb-Sossa, "Conclusion: Consejos y Advertencias," in Deeb-Sossa and Rodríguez, *Community-Based Participatory Research*, 230.

5. Research tip: Iris Morales, a member of the caucus and YLP, published an excellent source on this topic: *Through the Eyes of Rebel Women: The Young Lords; 1969–1976* (New York: Red Sugarcane Press, 2016).

6. Patricia Zavella, "Feminist Insider Dilemmas: Constructing Ethnic Identity with Chicana Informants," *Frontiers* 13, no. 3 (1993): 70.

7. Zavella, "Feminist Insider Dilemmas," 56.

8. Zavella, "Feminist Insider Dilemmas," 72.

9. Vicki L. Ruiz, "Situating Stories: The Surprising Consequences of Oral History," *Oral History Review* 25, no. 1–2 (Summer–Autumn 1998): 72.

10. Deeb-Sossa, "Conclusion," 236. See also L. Márquez, "Recovering Chicana/o Movement History," 94.

11. Edward D. Ives, *The Tape-Recorded Interview: A Manual for Fieldworkers in Folklore and Oral History* (Knoxville: University of Tennessee Press, 1974).

12. Ives, *Tape-Recorded Interview*, 39–40. Ives termed these "preliminary questions." Because in Chicanx and Latinx studies preliminary questions serve a very different function (as noted above, they are a critical part of initial interviewer-interviewee dialogues), in

our work the initial questions in the interview are termed "introductory."

13. Jonathan D. Moreno, *Undue Risk: Secret State Experiments on Humans* (New York: W. H. Freeman and Company, 2000), 79–80; Jonathan D. Moreno, "Goodbye to All That: The End of Moderate Protectionism in Human Subjects Research," *The Hastings Center Report* 31, no. 3 (2001): 10–11, https://doi.org/10.2307/3527549.

14. Joseph M. Verschaeve, "Scientific Racism and Human Rights Violations in Our Time: Tuskegee Must Never Be Forgotten," *Michigan Sociological Review* 22 (2008): 222, http://www.jstor.org/stable/40969147. See also Arthur L. Caplan, "When Evil Intrudes," *The Hastings Center Report* 22, no. 6 (1992): 29–32, https://doi.org/10.2307/3562946. See also Moreno, *Undue Risk*, 219–21, 248–49.

15. George J. Anna, "Anthropology, IRBs, and Human Rights," *American Ethnologist* 33, no. 4 (2006): 543, http://www.jstor.org/stable/4098888.

16. Note that the American Folklife Center also has useful information on how to conduct an oral history project. See https://loc.gov/folklife/familyfolklife/oralhistory.html.

17. Cindy O. Fierros and Dolores Delgado Bernal, "Vamos a Platicar: The Contours of Pláticas," *Chicana/Latina Studies* 15, no. 2 (Spring 2016): 103.

18. Fierros and Delgado Bernal, "Vamos a Platicar," 111.

19. Kathryn Blackmer Reyes and Julia Curry Rodríguez, "Testimonio: Origins, Terms, and Resources," in *Chicana/Latina Testimonios as Pedagogical, Methodological, and Activist Approaches to Social Justice*, ed. Dolores Delgado Bernal, Rebeca Burciaga, and Judith Flores Carmona (New York: Routledge, 2016), 162.

20. Bernal, Burciaga, and Carmona, introduction to *Chicana/Latina Testimonios*, i.

21. Blackmer Reyes and Curry Rodríguez, "Testimonio," 163.

22. Cinthya M. Saavedra, "Language and Literacy in the Borderlands: Acting upon the World Through 'Testimonios,'" *Language Arts* 88, no. 4 (2011): 262. See also Latina Feminist Group, *Telling to Live: Latina Feminist Testimonios* (Durham: Duke University Press, 2002), 13.

23. Saavedra, "Language and Literacy," 267.

24. Latina Feminist Group, *Telling to Live*, 13.

25. Latina Feminist Group, *Telling to Live*, 17.
26. Domitila Barrios de Chungara with Moema Viezzer, *Let Me Speak! Testimony of Domitila, a Woman of the Bolivian Mines*, trans. Victoria Ortiz (New York: Monthly Review Press, 1978).

CHAPTER 5

1. Maylei Blackwell, *¡Chicana Power! Contested Histories of Feminism in the Chicano Movement* (Austin: University of Texas Press, 2011), 28.
2. Gabriela González, *Redeeming La Raza: Transborder Modernity, Race, Respectability, and Rights* (New York: Oxford University, 2018), 165.
3. Anna Marie Sandoval, *Toward a Latina Feminism of the Americas* (Austin: University of Texas Press, 2008), 12.
4. G. González, *Redeeming La Raza*, 20.
5. Lorena V. Márquez, *La Gente: Struggles for Empowerment and Community Self-Determination in Sacramento* (Tucson: University of Arizona Press, 2020), 7.
6. L. Márquez, *La Gente*, 57.
7. Steven Osuna, "Obstinate Transnational Memories: How Oral Histories Shape Salvadoran-Mexican Subjectivities," in *U.S. Central Americans: Reconstructing Memories, Struggles, and Communities of Resistance*, ed. Karina O. Alvarado, Alicia Ivonne Estrada, and Ester E. Hernández (Tucson: University of Arizona Press, 2017), 88.
8. Miguel León-Portilla, *Aztec Thought and Culture*, trans. Jack Emory Davis (Norman: University of Oklahoma Press, 1963), 127.
9. Ester E. Hernández, "Remembering Through Cultural Interventions: Mapping Central Americans in L.A. Public Spaces," in Alvarado, Estrada, and Hernández, *U.S. Central Americans*, 156.
10. Elvia Rosales Arriola, "Amor y Esperanza: A Latina Lesbian Becomes a Law Professor," *Journal of Legal Education* 33, no. 3 (2017): 488.
11. Rose M. Borunda and Melissa Moreno, *Speaking from the Heart: Herstories of Chicana, Latina, and Amerindian Women*, 2nd ed. (Dubuque: Kendall Hunt, 2014), 70.
12. Gloria Anzaldúa, *Borderlands / La Frontera: The New Mestiza*, 4th ed. (San Francisco: Aunt Lute Press, 2007), 29.
13. Michael Nava, *Lay Your Sleeping Head* (San Francisco: Korima, 2016), 66.

14. Antonia I. Castañeda, "Gender, Race, and Culture: Spanish-Mexican Women in the Historiography of Frontier California," *Frontiers: A Journal of Women Studies* 11, no. 1 (1990): 11, https://doi.org/10.2307/3346697.

15. Sunshine Maria Anderson, "Defining an Alternative Discourse: A Look into Chicana/o Spaces Creating Identity, Resistance, and Healing Through Art and Music," in *El Mundo Zurdo 2: Selected Works from the 2010 Meeting of the Society for the Study of Gloria Anzaldúa*, ed. Sonia Saldívar-Hull, Norma Alarcón, and Rita E. Urquijo-Ruiz (San Francisco: Aunt Lute, 2012), 112.

16. Virginia Grise, *blu* (New Haven: Yale University, 2011), xvii.

17. Vanessa Ovalle Perez, "Toasting *México* in the American West: *Brindis* Poems and Political Loyalties of Women's Mexican Patriotic Clubs," *Letras Femeninas* 43, no. 1 (Summer–Fall 2017): 60, https://www.jstor.org/stable/10.14321/letrfeme.43.1.0060.

APPENDIX A

Because Chicago is the preferred style of the historian's profession, Dr. L Heidenreich wrote this section.

APPENDIX C

Because MLA is the preferred style of those who write in the fields of literature and culture, Dr. Urquijo-Ruiz wrote this section.

INDEX